"Postcolonial interpret  ine, know, and act ou of the empire. This mo one for those of us who are safely 'tenured' in (American!) imperial certitude and security. This readily accessible book helps us to understand the urgency of this move outside and provides categories through which we may reframe and resituate our theology. It is a most welcome starting point for a way of interpretation that is not a fad but a path to more responsible faith."

—Walter Brueggemann, Columbia Theological Seminary

"A ringing call to white Evangelicals to understand and abandon their cultural captivity. One need not embrace every argument to see that the basic message of this book is important and urgent."

—Ronald J. Sider, author of *Rich Christians in an Age of Hunger*

"It's too much to ask, I fear, that the people who most need *Decolonizing Evangelicalism* will actually read it. Too many of them have given their hearts to the Trump Klan and are too enthralled with *The Art of the Deal* to read anything else. But perhaps their children and grandchildren will dare to read this powerful book which unfolds as a conversation between two very insightful people with Evangelical roots, one white, one Native American. This book could change the next generation's understanding of what it means to be Christian, Evangelical, and American (or Canadian), and that would be good news indeed."

—Brian D. McLaren, author of *The Great Spiritual Migration*

Decolonizing
Evangelicalism

Decolonizing Evangelicalism

An 11:59 p.m. Conversation

Randy S. Woodley

and

Bo C. Sanders

foreword by
Grace Ji-Sun Kim

 CASCADE *Books* · Eugene, Oregon

DECOLONIZING EVANGELICALISM
An 11:59 p.m. Conversation

Cascade Books
An Imprint of Wipf and Stock Publishers
199 W. 8th Ave., Suite 3
Eugene, OR 97401

www.wipfandstock.com

PAPERBACK ISBN: 978-1-4982-9203-0
HARDCOVER ISBN: 978-1-4982-9205-4
EBOOK ISBN: 978-1-4982-9204-7

Cataloguing-in-Publication data:

Names: Woodley, Randy S., 1956–, author. | Sanders, Bo C., author. | Kim, Grace Ji-Sun, 1969–, foreword.

Title: Decolonizing evangelicalism : an 11:59 p.m. conversation / by Randy S. Woodley and Bo C. Sanders ; foreword by Grace Ji-Sun Kim.

Description: Eugene, OR : Cascade Books, 2020 | Includes bibliographical references.

Identifiers: ISBN 978-1-4982-9203-0 (paperback) | ISBN 978-1-4982-9205-4 (hardcover) | ISBN 978-1-4982-9204-7 (ebook)

Subjects: LCSH: Evangelicalism. | Religion and politics. | History—Imperialism and Colonialism. | History—Christianity. | Indians of North America—Religion. | Christianity and culture—North America. | Racism—Religious aspects—Christianity. | Reconciliation—Religious aspects—Christianity. | Race relations—Religious aspects—Christianity.

Classification: BL65.P7 W67 2020 (print) | BL65.P7 W67 (ebook)

Manufactured in the U.S.A.   02/24/20

Contents

Foreword

I WAS BORN IN Korea and immigrated to Canada in 1975. Korea, my home country, suffered under Japanese colonialism and empire from 1910 to 1945 while being ruled by military power. During this time my grandmother was attending school. Her and her classmates were given Japanese names and taught Japanese, never discussing the reasons as to why. While the children were not informed at school about what was happening, oppression was felt throughout the country. Colonialism is destructive: it destroys lives, culture, religion, and people—it nearly destroyed my antecedent bloodline. The effects of colonialism last for generations, as a country attempts to regain and reestablish its politics, history, culture, and identity.

During the period of Japanese rule, the people of Korea faced immeasurable injury. Numerous young girls were kidnapped from their families and forced to become "comfort women" for members of the Japanese army. The term "comfort women" was meant to describe those who today would be described as sex slaves. These women were stationed in different countries around Asia for the sole purpose of gratifying the sexual desires of the military. The statistics show upwards of two hundred thousand comfort women were held captive for the sexual satisfaction of the Japanese army. These comfort women served fifty to seventy men daily and as a result were often infected with venereal diseases. Being confined in cramped quarters with scarce medical attention led to illness, and after they got sick enough, they were killed. A whole generation of Korean women were brutally lost, disenfranchised, and disinherited due to colonial rule and imperial power.

Colonialism did not affect Korea only, as countless different instances of colonialism have made an enduring global impact in countries that are stuck under the dark legacy of their colonizers. Our world is complicated, intersectional, interrelated, intertwined, and imperialistic. Living under foreign rule forces change upon individuals and communities, who may never be able to fully regain the culture they once had. In understanding the impact of colonialism in our world, it becomes easier to recognize the extent to which it has affected the identity, religion, economy, and climate in a global context.

Given the large scope of colonialism's impact—it touches almost every aspect of our lives—to ignore it would be to ignore the problems of our society. Thus postcolonial theory aids many areas of study in understanding the complexities of the impact of colonialism on culture, society, and religion.

In theological studies we recognize the primary effect that colonialism has caused—damaged and destroyed lives. In response, postcolonial theology posits the need to decolonize. We need to detach ourselves from the harmful effects of imperialism and capitalism and work toward liberation and justice. In this significant book, *Decolonizing Evangelicalism*, theologians Randy Woodley and Bo Sanders take us with them as they show us the task of decolonizing theology. They point out that if Christianity is to be reflective of the life of Jesus, then colonial forms of Christianity cannot be considered to be Christian.

One of the tasks of theology is to liberate the individual and the community. But in so many ways, European theology, which has dominated much of Christian theology, has tended to grip our minds. Thus, it is urgent that we begin to free ourselves from academic theologies originating in Europe and the Americas. One way to begin this process is to be aware of theological voices around the globe and to listen to uncommon voices. Listening to such voices will illuminate how much the classical context determines our thoughts, ideas, and understandings.

In order to flourish in our present context, it is crucial that we recognize the voices of oppressed minorities—Native Americans, African Americans, Latin Americans, Asian Americans, womanists, feminists, LGBTQ and other voices that will deepen our theological understanding. Woodley and Sanders reveal how all these voices intersect and overlap with one another. They establish that it is our obligation to listen to diverse contemporary voices and work toward learning the nuances of social injustices so that as informed individuals we can share in finding solutions.

Woodley and Sanders also stress the importance of accepting many theologies as opposed to just one theology. This runs contrary to much of the history of Christian theology, which tried to produce a single voice created by white European men, leaving no room for other voices, for voices from the margins. This understanding has dominated much of Christian theology and only recently have we begun to recognize the importance of hearing several voices at once.

Furthermore, Woodley and Sanders emphasize that theology cannot be done in an ivory tower but must originate within our context and experiences. Theology must always be done in the trenches, so to speak, mindful of those in the grip of poverty, brokenness, hurt, and the structures of sin. Theology cannot hide these problems. Rather, it needs to tackle them and work within the brokenness of the people. This gives new life to theology and allows room for further growth and exploration.

Part of the task of theology is to work toward liberation, and not just for one group but for all. It is about giving life and meaning, rather than marginalization, oppression, and colonialism. Theology is about liberating and sustaining our goodness. It is a way to live out a life of shalom.

This timely book explores shalom and shows us that shalom is about love, justice, peace, and being inclusive of all people. Shalom is what all communities need to strive for to flourish and grow. Jesus insisted on equality, dignity, empowerment, and shalom community, which is a just community. Doing shalom encourages the community to come alive.

Shalom justice can be achieved if we work together and understand that everyone is our neighbor. Our mandate from God is to love our neighbor. Our neighbors are simply those around us, and as we recognize that we are all are interrelated, the command to "love thy neighbor" becomes much simpler to carry out. To love our neighbors means to love all people without prejudice. It means embracing those whom we fear or call foreigners.

In *Decolonizing Evangelicalism* Woodley and Sanders open our eyes to the global problems we face. This book serves as a window onto understanding our social ills and provides a realistic framework for how we can address and alleviate some of the problems plaguing our world. In our current cultural landscape, it is more important than ever to decolonize ourselves and to make our theologies both relevant and liberative. This innovative book sets out the task for us. Will you join me on this decolonizing theological journey toward shalom and justice for all?

—Grace Ji-Sun Kim

Preface

THE TERM *EVANGELICAL* HAS been used and misused for
centuries. Evangelicalism, in the more popular sense in
which we are using it, really dates back to the mid-nineteenth
century. The term is closely associated with evangelism,
especially through the work of evangelist (or "revivalist,"
as he was often called) Charles Finney. Finney developed a
series of methods, including protracted meetings, the anx-
ious bench, and calling people out by name from the pulpit,
that gained popularity in the latter part of the nineteenth
century and beyond (think Billy Graham). Revivalism and
evangelism became somewhat conflated over the years and
Evangelicalism was reborn anew.

By the time the modernist/fundamentalist schism was
in full swing in the early twentieth century, the people who
maintained what they thought were the fundamentals of
the Christian faith, including evangelism, were learning to
become comfortable with the name Evangelical. The advent
of parachurch organizations in the 1950s–1970s also led to

wider public use of the term *Evangelical*. The parachurch organizations were, by and large, nondenominational and as a group fell easily into this category. Although Evangelicalism has, by its own self-definition, conservative, centrist and progressive sides, the term has in the past several decades become associated in the larger public sphere with the prolife movement, anti-LGBTQ sentiment, and theological fundamentalism. In its popular sense, the term *Evangelicalism* describes a merger with politics resulting in a kind of civil religion and thus has become synonymous with support of conservative politics and the Republican Party.

Between them, the authors have more than fifty years working for and with Evangelical organizations. Having participated in conversations germane to the status of Evangelicalism for all these years, and having become critical of Evangelicalism's faults (which are many) and sympathetic to Evangelicalism's strengths, we felt it was time to broaden the conversation, not as a last-ditch effort to save a dying movement—for history will be the judge of where the movement goes from here—but as an attempt to help others to understand it, as we try to understand it, through precolonial, postcolonial, decolonial and anticolonial lenses. While there is much to shed, there is also much to savor in Evangelicalism's history. Our hope is simply to allow others to find a place in the conversation before the movement evolves into its next form or ends completely.

Authors' Bios/Social Location

It seems important to us, and fair to you, to introduce ourselves and our own social locations from the very beginning of this conversation. Our goal is to help you find a place in this conversation, along with us, as we dialogue together. The authors have been sharing this conversation together in one way or another for the past thirteen years. In 2018 we began a weekly podcast, *Peacing It All Together*, that would invite others to join a wider conversation about this and other important topics; we call it a "journey place." We are happy you have chosen to take this part of the journey with us!

Bo Sanders

Bo was born in Ohio, learned to talk in Georgia, was raised in Chicago and went to high school in Saskatchewan, Canada, where he became a dual citizen. He married a girl from Montana; the two of them moved to New York for a year and then went to college in Redding, California. Their first church was in Saratoga Springs, New York, and before Claremont, California, where Bo did his doctoral work, they lived in the Pacific Northwest, where Bo got his master's degree in Portland. They have been married for twenty-three years. Life and ministry have led them on adventures in more than twenty-two countries.

Bo's parents were dairy farmers when he was born and were soon called to ministry. They pastored with the Free Methodist denomination in suburban Chicago before his dad became a seminary professor while Bo was in high school. He followed his parents into ministry and was ordained with the Christian & Missionary Alliance denomination. His eighteen years of pastoral ministry have provided him a lifetime of stories.

Most recently he helped start an innovative conversational community in Los Angeles while working on a PhD in Practical Theology (with a concentration in Religious Education). His dissertation is a case study on Wesleyan distinctives and the Methodist tradition that have resulted in racial, ethnic, and gender diversity for United Methodist Church leadership. Bo employs critical race theory as his lens in the hope of helping congregations and communities address issues related to Whiteness in the midst of changing demographics and related cultural shifts.

Bo wrote his master's thesis with Randy as his mentor at George Fox Evangelical Seminary (now Portland Seminary), where he is currently employed as a visiting professor of theology. Bo is a large, able-bodied, straight, white, middle-class man who tries to learn about being human and being a follower of Jesus from people who are none of those things.

Randy Woodley

Randy Woodley is a first-generation college-educated, straight, light-skinned, Native American male, born in 1956. Randy has spent his career working with people from backgrounds similar to his own, the poor and marginalized of society, but toward the end of his career he has found himself in the erudite world of academia. His family roots are in the Deep South, Michigan and Oklahoma. Randy was raised in a blue-collar, working poor community called Willow Run, southeast of Detroit, Michigan. He holds (reluctantly) a BA, an MDiv, and a PhD in the area of intercultural studies, and is known as a public theologian, speaker, coach, and teacher. Randy is a legal descendant of the United Keetoowah Band of Cherokee Indians in Oklahoma and has always clung to an American Indian identity. Both his parents are from mixed-blood Cherokee Indian and White lineage.

Randy's father is one of nine children who were raised on a small farm in rural Mississippi. His father has a twelfth-grade education, is a World War II veteran and worked most of his life in a company he started as a carpenter/homebuilder. Randy's mother has an eighth-grade education. As the eldest daughter in a family of ten, it was necessary for her to quit school and move to the city to work and send money home to her family. She spent most of her career as a beautician. On his maternal side, Randy is a first-generation non-coal miner; his maternal grandfather was instrumental in establishing the United Mine Workers in central Alabama.

Most of Randy's life of service has been spent among both traditional and Christian Native American communities, where he has endeavored to empower the most disenfranchised people in America. Randy and his wife, Edith, an Eastern Shoshone tribal member, have four grown children and four grandchildren at the time of this writing. They cosustain an Indigenous, regenerative farm, seed company, community, and school south of Portland, Oregon.

Randy has founded or cofounded several grassroots organizations, including Cross Cultural Concerns, Christians for Justice, the North American Institute for Indigenous Theological Studies, Evangelicals 4 Justice, the Eloheh Indigenous Center for Earth Justice, Eagle's Wings Ministry, and Eloheh Village for Indigenous Leadership. He also served on the Portland Area Native American Climate Council and on the Oregon Department of Education American Indian/Alaska Native Advisory Council.

Randy teaches full-time at Portland Seminary in Portland, Oregon, as Distinguished Professor of Faith and Culture and Director of Intercultural and Indigenous Studies. Some of his other books include *The Harmony Tree: A Story of Healing and Community* (Friesen); *Shalom and the Community of Creation: An Indigenous Vision* (Eerdmans); and *Living in Color: Embracing God's Passion for Ethnic Identity* (InterVarsity). In addition, he has published dozens of book chapters and magazine/journal articles.

Introduction

WHY SHOULD YOU LISTEN to our conversation? Everywhere we go people are asking a question that many Evangelicals are afraid to discuss, namely, Is Evangelicalism dead? Honestly, sometimes the question is not a question at all but a proclamation: "Evangelicalism is dead." We know what that means is, "Evangelicalism is dead *to me!*" The two of us come to the conversation steeped in Evangelical traditions. We are not strangers to the subject at hand, nor are we quite ready to make a similar declaration without looking deeper into the conversation. We hope you will join us on the journey as we take a very honest look at Evangelicalism and, by default, Christianity in America.

Over the years, the two of us have had a running dialogue about a great many things. Since both of us are theologically trained, we talk a lot about God, the church, our world, peace, justice, truth, and especially how these affect Evangelicalism, the particular "theological camp" in which we were trained. Though it may seem like we are coming from the same place (and honestly, how could that lead to true dialogue?), the truth is we come from different backgrounds, and perhaps our conversations are strengthened by our diversity. One of us is old(er) and the other young(er). One is situated in an urban setting and the other has adopted a rural lifestyle. Both of us have been pastors of Evangelical congregations but in different denominations and in different parts of the country. We have both taught at Evangelical institutions, but each of us has been seen as introducing new voices into the academy. Also, and importantly, one of us identifies as White and the other as Indigenous, so we have been informed by very different worldviews. True, we are both straight and male, and—at the time of this writing, at least—we both live in the Pacific Northwest, but really, there is enough diversity to find meaningful dialogue between just the two of us. But most of all we hope our conversation is just a catalyst for you, the reader—an introduction and an invitation to take what we have started and continue it, speaking and listening through many different perspectives.

One of the immediate concerns we share is the type of political stance many Evangelicals, especially White Evangelicals, took during the past presidential election—we find it baffling, frankly. Whereas large numbers of Black, Latino, and Asian American Evangelicals chose not to support Donald J. Trump, more than 81 percent of White Evangelicals voted for him—a man who has shown himself to be definitely, unapologetically misogynistic, racist, and xenophobic and who displays a complete disregard for the natural world. What further baffles us (and perhaps you too) is the fact that well into his first term, President Trump has only gotten worse, making even more outrageous statements that reveal his prejudices, and in spite of this fact his Evangelical support has not wavered.

To watch Evangelicals "hitch their wagon to Trump's star" is perplexing, to say the least. This support comes at a time when Evangelicals, like many other Christians in America, are leaving the church in significant numbers and dropping the name "Evangelical." It is no overstatement to say that Evangelicalism today has become synonymous with being White, conservative and, likely, Republican. This examination of Evangelicalism is an attempt to understand the mindset of Evangelicalism in this current time of crisis from a decolonial and theological perspective.

It should be said from the start that Evangelicals are not new to the political arena, even though they may have approached the issues from different perspectives in the past. Historical figures in the nineteenth century like Charles Grandison Finney, Jonathan Blanchard, Angelina and Sarah Grimké, Theodore Weld, Orange Scott, Evan Jones, Jesse Bushyhead, and many others who could rightly be called Evangelicals were very actively involved in American politics, or at least in raising social awareness, through their words and actions. Using the political system, nineteenth-century Evangelicals fought determinedly against slavery and institutional racism, and they advocated for Native American rights, women's rights, temperance, and other causes.

And yet, something has changed—today's Evangelicals could be characterized, arguably, as taking the opposite side in these political exchanges from their historical cousins.

Many of today's Evangelicals have trouble supporting the rights of women, African Americans, Native Americans, and immigrants, not to mention a whole host of issues involving human dignity that seem to reflect biblical values. So what changed? With the advent of the twentieth century came a great schism among Christians in America. What has become known as the fundamentalist/modernist split created a strange and unhealthy binary: Christians had to choose whether to read the Bible literally or to use various interpretive methods such as form, historic, and textual criticism. Science became the friend of some and the enemy of others. Evangelicalism continued to raise its head at various times during the century-long debate as a sort of middle position, but slightly to the right of center. Education was of primary importance to Evangelicals, but so was remaining faithful to the Scriptures.

In 1973 a group of concerned Evangelicals came together in Chicago for the purpose of rededicating Evangelicalism to social action. Out of this meeting came the Chicago Declaration of Evangelical Social Concern, which we quote here in its entirety.

Chicago Declaration of Evangelical Social Concern

November 25, 1973, Chicago, Illinois

As evangelical Christians committed to the Lord Jesus Christ and the full authority of the Word of God, we affirm that God lays total claim upon the lives of his people. We cannot, therefore, separate our lives from the situation in which God has placed us in the United States and the world.

We confess that we have not acknowledged the complete claim of God on our lives.

We acknowledge that God requires love. But we have not demonstrated the love of God to those suffering social abuses.

We acknowledge that God requires justice. But we have not proclaimed or demonstrated his justice to an unjust American society. Although the Lord calls us to defend the social and economic rights of the poor and oppressed, we have mostly remained silent. We deplore the historic involvement of the church in America with racism and the conspicuous responsibility of the evangelical community for perpetuating the personal attitudes and institutional structures that have divided the body of Christ along color lines. Further, we have failed to condemn the exploitation of racism at home and abroad by our economic system.

We affirm that God abounds in mercy and that he forgives all who repent and turn from their sins. So we call our fellow evangelical Christians to demonstrate repentance in a Christian discipleship that confronts the social and political injustice of our nation.

We must attack the materialism of our culture and the maldistribution of the nation's wealth and services. We recognize that as a nation we play a crucial role in the imbalance and injustice of international trade and development. Before God and a billion hungry neighbors, we must rethink our values regarding our present standard of living and promote a more just acquisition and distribution of the world's resources.

We acknowledge our Christian responsibilities of citizenship. Therefore, we must challenge the misplaced trust of the nation in economic and military might—a proud trust that promotes a national pathology of war and violence which victimizes our neighbors at home and abroad. We must resist the temptation to make the nation and its institutions objects of near-religious loyalty.

We acknowledge that we have encouraged men to prideful domination and women to irresponsible passivity. So we call both men and women to mutual submission and active discipleship.

> We proclaim no new gospel, but the Gospel of our Lord Jesus Christ who, through the power of the Holy Spirit, frees people from sin so that they might praise God through works of righteousness.
>
> By this declaration, we endorse no political ideology or party, but call our nation's leaders and people to that righteousness which exalts a nation.
>
> We make this declaration in the biblical hope that Christ is coming to consummate the Kingdom and we accept his claim on our total discipleship until he comes.

Notice the concern in the Chicago Declaration for justice, racial equality, poverty, hunger, equitable trade agreements, anti-militarism, and women's rights, among other causes. Those who signed the Chicago Declaration were attempting to bring a more robust, holistic gospel to America and the world, and many of them have become almost legendary in their commitment to their cause.[1] Another contemporary attempt of that era, in a direction similar to that of the Chicago Declaration, was made in Lausanne, Switzerland, at the first International Congress

---

1. Signers included John F. Alexander, Joseph Bayly, Ruth L. Bentley, William Bentley, Dale Brown, James C. Cross, Donald Dayton, Roger Dewey, James Dunn, Daniel Ebersole, Samuel Escobar, Warren C. Falcon, Frank Gaebelein, Sharon Gallagher, Theodore E. Gannon, Art Gish, Vernon Grounds, Nancy Hardesty, Carl F. H. Henry, Paul B. Henry, Clarence Hilliard, Walden Howard, Rufus Jones, Robert Tad Lehe, William Leslie, C. T. McIntire, Wes Michaelson, David O. Moberg, Stephen Mott, Richard Mouw, David Nelson, F. Burton Nelson, William Pannell, John Perkins, William Petersen, Richard Pierard, Wyn Wright Potter, Ron Potter, Bernard Ramm, Paul Rees, Boyd Reese, Joe Roos, James Robert Ross, Eunice Schatz, Ronald J. Sider, Donna Simons, Lewis Smedes, Foy Valentine, Marlin Van Elderen, Jim Wallis, Robert Webber, Merold Westphal and John Howard Yoder.

Lausanne covenant

on World Evangelization. There were several subsequent Lausanne conferences but only the initial conference fully broke through with a resounding message for Evangelical social concerns. Education, too, became a means for propagating the Evangelical message of social justice as a necessary part of everyday Christian life. For instance, one squarely Evangelical seminary, Eastern Baptist Theological Seminary, took as its motto "The whole gospel for the whole world." Sociologists, church historians, and political analysts will have much to add to the conversation when asking the question, What happened to the social concern and social activism of Evangelicalism?

With each move toward promoting social justice came equal and opposite reactions from others claiming to be Evangelicals. Recently, more than four thousand religious leaders have declared "social justice" to be anti-Evangelical![2] We would like to use a decolonial and constructionist theological lens in our attempt to answer the question posed above. As we have a conversation that provides alternatives to thinking about contemporary forms of Evangelicalism, we hope you will join us and expand the conversation to your dialogue partners, churches, educational institutions and other venues.

In order to establish a context for our discussion, we would like to introduce you to the broader conversation concerning decolonial, postcolonial and anticolonial theologies surrounding the concerns over what could be seen as "the fall of Evangelicalism." Notice we use the plural "theologies" because "theology" (singular) implies there is

2. For an evaluation of this troubling development within Evangelicalism, see the following blog post: Libby Anne, "On John MacArthur's (Very Racist) Statement on Social Justice," http://www.patheos.com/blogs/lovejoyfeminism/2018/09/on-john-macarthurs-racist-statement-on-social-justice/.

only one narrative, which is a very colonial presumption. For example, postcolonial theology (singular) implies that postcolonial theologies are an established theological field, which they are not. As we move toward defining what can be broadly interpreted as a dialogue concerning postcolonial theologies, and throughout the course of this brief introductory book, we will offer you several definitions of postcolonial theologies, but first we would like to get you thinking about a few very important things.

Postcolonial theologies are not always easily defined, and that is part of the problem of discussing them. In attempting to define postcolonial theologies we realize that postcolonial theologies are diverse and fluid, allowing for a great variety of thought and interpretation and requiring ongoing conversation. We think that doing postcolonial theologies is not so much about arriving at a sealed and protected definition as it is about a journey. On this journey, however, there is a definite point of departure, namely, colonized theological thinking, particularly as it has been applied in Evangelicalism, which we will say more about later. So, where will this journey take us? And how do we describe the landscape of a place we are moving toward but have never been to? Consider this: the important questions underlying postcolonial theologies do not concern what postcolonial theologies *are* but rather what postcolonial theologies *do*. Get ready for the first solid answer to the problem we have presented. What postcolonial theologies *do*, first and foremost, is this: they *deconstruct*. What do they deconstruct?

The Deconstruction Zone

Decolonial, postcolonial, and anticolonial theologies critique and deconstruct theologies of empire.[3] All imperial

3. We have chosen not to draw a sharp distinction between the

Christian theologies, we will argue, surfaced at least as early as the fourth century, with the conversion to Christianity of Constantine and the Roman Empire.[4] Theologies of empire made their début in the writings of church fathers such as Ambrose, Jerome, Cyprian, and especially Augustine, the Christian theologian with arguably the most influence in

concepts of imperialism and empire. Instead we use them somewhat interchangeably throughout this conversation because both lead to the same destructive patterns and theologies of conquest. However, we would like to note that we understand that settler colonialism is the result of empire-driven agencies, including the church, who seek to impose an external and unnatural grid of colonial patterns over nature and over the Indigenous peoples that have developed over time. The presumption of empire is that this imposed grid will create profit, and it is often justified by the false logic that people groups understood to be different (or foreign, or alien) will be better off in the end under the colonizer's subjugation.

4. Edward Schillebeeckx, in his book *The Church with a Human Face*, points out that the original Jesus movement was egalitarian and most likely similar in form to a loose congregationalism governed (at least by AD 100 or so) by egalitarian groups but never without leadership—originally apostolic and later connected by evangelists and prophets—and always organized at some level. Schillebeeckx points out that by AD 100–120 Ignatius of Antioch had contextualized church structure around the military organization of imperial Roman occupied lands that organized administration around diocese and parishes—with the bishop equaling the field general. But in Alexandria, up until the early third century, the church was ruled by coequal boards (a council of elders as well as a council of youngers) in a generally democratic format—so that there were at least two completely different forms of organization. It was under Cyprian (late 300s) that the church took its more or less Western form, which has been accepted as the norm in Western Christianity. Like so many other forms of contextualization, it was their idea of contextualization in their own context, but they normalized and universalized their context to fit the whole world. Also notice that what later became titles holding demonstrable authority like *episcopoi* and *presbyteroi* were likely better understood as functional titles in the early church. Sincere thanks to Greg Leffel for pointing out this invaluable resource.

church history. It was Augustine who formulated perhaps the most famous of imperial theologies, that of the just war, in various works, including his *City of God*. Today's imperial theologies are subtler than they were in the past, but they are all around us, being embedded within what we have blindly followed as *normative* Christianity. To make a stand against what have become such unassuming theologies embedded within empire is to oppose empire. Historically, those who oppose empire suffer a loss of popularity with establishment (imperial) theologians, who are usually in the majority. The task of deconstruction is one that requires courage. Because you are reading this book, you may be among those showing the kind of courage it takes to oppose the amalgamation of Christianity and empire that we still experience as normative in Evangelical Christianity today.

If you have attempted to read much in the way of post-colonial theology, you know that one of the frightful aspects that readers often encounter is how seemingly complex the language surrounding the subject can be. Such academic language, although employed with good intention, betrays an inherent problem in the writing of decolonial, postcolonial, and anticolonial theologies. Theologies whose aim is first to deconstruct cannot usually be written well "from above," meaning by those situated within the most learned of Western academic traditions, who may be representing a classist approach. Such theologies should not be written from the proverbial ivory tower. We have done our best to dialogue and avoid classism, but like everyone, we too wear blinders at times.

The task of these postcolonial theologies is not to reflect the tools of empire by imitating the classism of empire, nor is it to create another category of language for a special class of postcolonial theologians. No, postcolonial theologies must be written for the people and in the language of the people. In other words, postcolonial theologies should be written *from* and *for* those who have been most negatively affected by empire. Therefore, it is important for you to understand, as much as possible, who is writing any particular postcolonial theology and to identify the social location of those who claim to be postcolonial theologians. None of us should fool ourselves by believing our social location does not affect our own particular slant on this or any other subject. It is for this reason that the two of us provided some information about ourselves and our social location earlier, in the Preface. We want you to know where we are coming from before we get too far along on the journey.

Reconstruction, Really?

After asking what postcolonial theologies *do* (and after identifying the social location of the authors), the next thing you may want to consider while reading any book on decolonial, postcolonial, or anticolonial theologies—or any book, period—is *how these theologies do reconstruction.* There are no set rules for reconstruction, but we think perhaps that is a good thing. The reconstructive process is like that unknown place we mentioned earlier, so we can't actually be certain of how our postcolonial theologies will re-form themselves. There are, however, tools at our disposal that will guide the process of forming postcolonial theologies, and that, we hope, is the point of this book. Consider yourself on a journey with us as we discover together what still remains—and, to a degree (because God is *the* Great Mystery), will always remain—uncharted territory.

1

Was Jesus an Evangelical, or Even Perhaps a Postcolonial Theologian?

Bo: Since Evangelicalism is supposed to be all about Jesus, how do we understand Jesus in light of empire?

Randy: Jesus never became a Christian of any kind. That might sound funny or obvious, but it is an important point we should remember. Jesus was a first-century Jew who lived all his life under the occupation of perhaps one of the most oppressive and powerful empires in history. You might assume Jesus would have been affected by this powerful empire that was constantly bearing down on him, but instead Jesus displayed a remarkably decolonized mind. Jesus did not accommodate the Roman conquerors, except to include them, along with the rest of the cosmos, as potential recipients of the good news in a theology of salvation/healing. Jesus' understanding of salvation/healing appeared to be much more holistic and all-encompassing than that of many of the people within his own religion at that time. Perhaps Jesus' theology and worldview was larger in scope than the world his contemporaries could have imagined, a fact that would eventually lead to his death.

Bo: I noticed you use the words "salvation" and "healing" kind of interchangeably. Was that intentional?

Randy: Very much so. I think the word *salvation* has too much baggage to continue to be used theologically.

Bo: What do you mean by that?

Randy: Well, the word itself speaks of the illegitimate power claimed by the church, which, whether through force or influence, has held the world hostage to its demands concerning its ability to grant salvation or, if you will, *paradise*. If you hold the "keys to the kingdom," you get to decide not only who gets in but what they have to do to get there. I don't think Jesus ever intended the concept of salvation to be associated with that kind of illegitimate power. Only Creator has that power, and Creator offers it to everyone, regardless of their affiliation with the established church. Although I've studied the languages, I'm not a Hebrew or Greek scholar, but I have heard some scholars suggest that the word *healing* conveys a more accurate meaning than *salvation* in much of Scripture. I certainly believe it is a better theological choice. Healing is a process that requires our cooperation. I think of a few teachings like, "Now is our [healing] much closer than when we first began," or when Jesus said, "[Healing] has come to this home today, for this man has shown himself to be a true son of Abraham." Creator offers healing to the whole world—to the whole planet.

Bo: Are there other words you think are baggage-laden and need to be rethought?

Randy: Absolutely! I actually have a list. I think I'm up to about a dozen of what I consider to be harmful word constructs, particularly as they are used by Evangelicals. We form these social categories that become laden with bias. The Evangelical church has done that, and I think that, at minimum, it is time for re-verbiaging some of the language.

Bo: Re-verbiaging?

Randy: Yeah, I actually made that word up just now [*laughter*]. Anyway, are you ready for the list of words on which I'd love to issue a moratorium?

Bo: I hope so!

Randy: These are some of the words imbued with the baggage of Christian, and especially Evangelical, empire: *God, Christian, Bible, kingdom, missionary, gospel, salvation, heathen, repent, sin, born-again, crusade, ministry,* and especially, *Evangelical!*

Bo: Whoa! Those are some major concepts.

Randy: Absolutely, and the Evangelical church needs to make major changes, so maybe this would be a good starting place. Here are some suggestions for replacements or, as I said earlier, "re-verbiaging" [*laughter*]. And note, my suggestions are just that, *my* suggestions. There are likely other substitutions that work better than these, but these words reflect my own theology, which, I have to admit, is pretty simple. *God* becomes "Creator" or "Great Mystery"; *Christian* becomes "a follower of Jesus or the Jesus Way"; *Bible* becomes "Scriptures"; *kingdom* becomes "community of creation"; *missionary* becomes "ambassador"; *gospel* becomes "good news"; *salvation* becomes "healing"; *heathen* is thrown out completely; *repent* becomes "turn around"; *sin* becomes "mistake" or, when used as a verb, "fail"; *crusade* becomes simply "a meeting"; ministry becomes "service"; and *Evangelical* becomes "Jesus-woke." It's not rocket science; it's just simply rethinking our biased categories that have fed into our poor theologies.

Bo: Wow! All I can say is, thanks for that, and I'm sure there will be some people who have a problem with it!

Randy: And there are a lot of people who have a problem with Evangelicalism too, right?

Bo: I can't argue with that. Let me continue asking you about Jesus and empire.

Randy: Okay. So, in light of Jesus' experience as one who never gave into the theologies of empire, we should ask again, what are these postcolonial-type theologies? Put simply, it seems to me that postcolonial theologies are all-inclusive theologies that decenter any empire-perpetuating force seeking to establish itself as superior to, and centered above, anyone and anything else. Postcolonial theologies, by their nature, should not only lift up the disenfranchised and marginalized but also restore theological equity and, to a degree, theological equality, which was displayed throughout the life and teachings of Jesus. Jesus refused to accept an assumed colonial existence. And he did not condone the goals of empire. In fact, Jesus' whole life and message were resolutely set against empire. Because he was against empire, we may refer to Jesus as a (and perhaps *the*) foundational example of a postcolonial theologian.

Bo: How do you think understanding Jesus as against empire could be helpful to Evangelicalism?

Randy: Jesus, as seen through an Evangelical (imperial) Christian hermeneutical lens, is *the savior of the world and one's own personal Lord and savior.* This particular theological lens has formed much of the basis of modern Western Evangelical Christianity and mission. In modern Evangelical theological interpretation, this very abstract narrative of Christ was used as a colonizing force, promoting imperial Christianity and removing the freedoms of many, many people, including Indigenous people all over the world. But to a degree, this narrow reading of Jesus as simply *the savior* limits everyone's freedom.

Bo: How so?

Randy: We limit Jesus—or maybe a better way to say it is we try to control Jesus by limiting our theological image of him, and people who try to live for Jesus end up with a very limited imagination concerning what Creator expects and what is possible in our world. Evangelicals, often without meaning it, have become great at religious oppression. To be completely honest, I think that particular theological lens is a form of idolatry in that it re-creates God in our limited image.

Bo: Can you think of ways this has been done in the past?

Randy: Sure. That narrow focus of the church granting the dispensation of Jesus as primarily a savior and ticket to heaven who becomes the "conquering Christ" of empire, and then adapting its theology to become a missiology of empire, subjugated the very lives of Indigenous and other peoples around the world, who found themselves victims of Christian colonization. From early on Christian theology and missiology have had everything to do with the human use and misuse of power. Evangelicals know the gospel is supposed to be about love, but that kind of love cannot integrate with power; real love and power over the other is a true binary. In spite of the impossibility, the two strange bedfellows of *love and power* now seem to be almost always entangled in Evangelicalism's theological and actionable reach. Love as expressed by Jesus and the use of power over others are simply incompatible. The juxtaposition of love and power is a false balance in light of the story of incarnation, the message given by Jesus and the life he lived. According to Jesus, power is to be given over to others who do not have it. The structured order, or government of God's love, is not power over others but rather is based on the ancient system of shalom.

The Relationship of Shalom to Postcolonial Theologies

Bo: How do you understand shalom?

Randy: Shalom is an ancient Israeli construct concretizing practical love to be expressed through structures and systems. The structured order, or government of God's love, is shalom and is related to the constructs in Scripture concerning Sabbath and Jubilee.

Bo: So, this is a big-picture idea?

Randy: Very big picture in that it is a construct in Scripture from beginning to end, and the kingdom of which Jesus taught is a shalom kingdom. Shalom is seen in the beauty and balance of the Genesis creation stories. Shalom, as seen against the background of God's good intentions, is broken at almost every level in the stories of Genesis 3–11. These examples of broken shalom include the breaks between God and humanity, between marriage partners, between the earth/creation and humanity, between siblings, in civil society and between neighbors. If we do not understand the big-picture shalom construct there is no way we are going to understand the words and life of Jesus. Again, the kingdom Jesus spoke of is a shalom kingdom or a kingdom based on the values and principles of shalom—what I call the "community of creation."[1]

Bo: You mentioned marginalized people earlier—can you talk about that?

Randy: Shalom also creates room for the poor, disenfranchised, and marginalized to receive empowerment in such cases as widows, orphans, and foreigners but in a structured way. Ancient Israel's structured shalom left food out for others during the harvest; set aside portions of land to be harvested by those who didn't own land and for the wild animals; and held feasts that include everyone at the same table. Shalom is God's community of creation or counterkingdom of inclusion to a power-based empire of exclusion. And notice, this is not just about humanity. Creator

1. "Community of creation" is an expression used to convey the understanding that all things created are rooted in a symbiotic relationship with each other and with Creator. Like Creator, we are never alone. The whole life system, and each part, whether it be the ecosystem, the solar system, or the multiverse, serves a purpose in the community of creation. Understanding the relatedness of all things to each other is helpful in understanding our human purpose within the whole. The danger of the system occurs when we study the specific parts of creation and we forget the context of the whole and our interdependent relationship to the whole community of creation. The whole community of creation includes both unity and diversity, from the smallest subatomic particle to the human body to the multiverse. Homogeneity is not a permanent ontological state of being but diversity with unity is both a fluctuating state and is the essence of ontological permanence. The foundation of all life is found in both unity and diversity. The foundation for living according to the ways of the Community of Creator must include the recognition and appreciation of both unity and diversity, which is part of God's shalom empire of love.

cares for all the creatures of the earth and the earth itself. The shalom kingdom is the Empire of Love.

Bo: That seems like a lot to unpack, but can you say more?

Randy: Creator's love is abundant, including peace, mercy, justice, hospitality, righteousness, restitution, and a whole plethora of characteristics and expressions for the common good. Shalom is the ethic Jesus preached and the action he lived as he confronted systems of broken shalom in a fragmented world. The "kingdom" Jesus referred to again and again is the shalom kingdom, which is not ethereal or utopian in nature but very real. Shalom can be clearly identified and it is communal in nature; it is not satisfied to seek the good of the individual alone. Shalom seeks the common good, and it benefits the whole community in identifiable and tangible ways.

Bo: I know you are looking at the big picture and minimizing the idea of shalom for individuals, but as a very individualistic society, if we want to begin to participate in shalom on a personal level, how do we begin?

Randy: One very visible path to shalom is when we engage in hospitality, which shalom provides even to one's enemies. Shalom hospitality leads to understanding others who may be different from ourselves. Understanding others leads to acceptance of both our commonalities and differences. Acceptance of the differences leads to caring. Caring leads to community actions that create systems for the well-being of the whole community based in equity, justice, and equality. These systems and structures provide shalom living, and individuals do benefit from the systems in place, as I said, because individual well-being becomes the by-product of shalom. Indigenous peoples in America, and all over much of the world, also have a shalom-type construct that I refer to in a general sense as the Harmony Way. These systems and structures provide for harmonious (shalom) living.[2] In fact, I have come to believe that the Harmony Way and the values that are derived from it are the original instructions given to humankind—instructions the world needs desperately.

Bo: So, to kind of summarize, what is the connection between love, power, shalom, postcolonial theologies, and Evangelicalism?

Randy: Jesus said, "Love your enemies." I don't think Jesus simply meant for us not to hate our enemies. That seems to be where most Evangelicals are comfortable leaving things: "Just don't be a hater." But the opposite of love is not in fact hate. Hatred implies an emotional investment, meaning that we actually care about the people we hate, right? Hate has to be maintained and is often driven by passion. We just hate to admit we have emotional investment in those we claim to hate. No, the opposite of love is not hate. The binary opposite of love is apparent in such attitudes as indifference, superficiality, disconnectedness, presumed superiority, and individualism. Jesus said we are to love our enemies, meaning that we should not ignore them, or treat them superficially, or disconnect from them emotionally, or think of ourselves as superior to them, thus creating a distance. Nor should we merely be concerned about our individual selves. Jesus' admonition to love our enemies was inspiring, imaginative, and entirely ingenious.

Bo: In what ways can we help people understand more about loving our enemies?

---

2. See Woodley, *Shalom and the Community of Creation: An Indigenous Vision.*

Randy: Loving our enemies requires, at minimum, listening to them. When we really listen to people we consider different, or what I call "the cultural other," we realize that their humanity is not so different from our own and that we share many commonalities. I think we share a common humanity with our enemies when we listen to them. I think listening bestows dignity. The next stage in the process is to learn to accept the differences between us and then, eventually, appreciate and even learn to celebrate those differences. The hopeful theological realization will be that we have been placed in a whole community of creation that is all-encompassing and in which there is a place for everyone, even our enemies. Jesus' strategy does away with us-and-them scenarios and always creates the vital and communal *we*. The posture of Jesus' love was living in vulnerability, and in order to do postcolonial theology well, I think we, too, must become vulnerable.

Bo: So, you were summarizing, but at the very end you slipped in another big theological concept. You said we all must become vulnerable. Is that, perhaps, the stuff of real love?

Randy: Exactly! How can we love if we don't become vulnerable? You can't even build a good marriage on that, though many people try, much less build a model for the whole world. Although God's nature is quite unfathomable, in Jesus we are able to get some glimpses of some very concrete aspects of Great Mystery. Could it be that God is the most vulnerable *being* that exists? If God is love, and love means being vulnerable, then God must represent the essence of vulnerability. The incarnation of Jesus expressed Great Mystery's vulnerability. Jesus' lifestyle of hanging out with the poor and marginalized expressed Creator's vulnerability. The crucifixion demonstrated God's vulnerability. Jesus' sharing

Creator's mission with us, and leaving the responsibility in our hands to act with God by structuring love as shalom, is a radical expression of a most vulnerable Creator God.

Bo: And you are saying that this was the message of Jesus?

Randy: In Jesus, we are invited to become fellow human beings with others who are different from us: to exchange and empower dignity in ourselves and others; to join in reciprocal conversion of each other's understanding of truth; and to live with, for, and among the community of creation, including people, in shalom. This is one of the lessons of the story Jesus told of the prodigal son in Luke 15. The watching father made himself vulnerable to the wayward son. The opposite of vulnerability is control, including the illegitimate use of power. The misuse of power is among the primary failures of colonization and it has, unfortunately, often been justified through colonial theologies embedded in empire, particularly Evangelicalism.

Mission

Bo: One of the questions that always comes up among the critique of Evangelicalism is evangelism. How do you understand evangelism or God's mission?

Randy: God's mission (the *missio Dei*), meaning that God has a mission to bring everyone and *everything* in creation (the community of creation) back to a shalom existence, happens because God is love. Shalom is an ethic of love, and, as mentioned, it is love that is deliberately structured for the common good of all people. Shalom systems are built on very practical love. It is actually a form of love that can be built into systemic governance. Dismantling systems of oppression, especially those that have been justified by imperial theologies, should be the first work of postcolonial theologies because relieving people's suffering is based in love. Shalom, a practical outworking of God's mission on earth, is the guideline for the reconstructive process. So, what are the first steps of shalom?

Again, hospitality is a major part of living out shalom. Hospitality is tangible love. Intentional hospitality is God's mission through Jesus and it is our mission to others. Hospitality can be expressed as hospitable relief or as hospitable development or as both, but it is only "mission" when one acts like Jesus as the hospitable host or even as the gracious and honest guest.

Postcolonial conversations don't relish the idea of evangelism or mission, but I feel like living a missional life means intentionally reminding ourselves and others, through our actions and, as needed, our words, that we are a "homing device" for Creator's love—for Creator's vulnerability and Creator's acceptance. I think postcolonial theologies can be inherently missional as they are moving against empire, not just in their critique or deconstructive process; they are creating postcolonial lifestyles by replacing the inhospitality of colonial oppressors with hospitable shalom. Replacing evil with good is one way to decenter, destabilize, decommission, and destroy the structures that work for empire and then reimagine and replace them with structures that empower everyone equally through love.

Bo: So, to put it concisely?

Randy: Love can be the essence of postcolonial mission. Love is expressed structurally through shalom. The first step of shalom is vulnerability in welcoming people, especially those different from us, through hospitality.

Justice

Bo: Okay, let's turn to the harsher realities of love—what about justice?

Randy: In much of my reading of postcolonial theologies it seems justice is the central motif. So, you're right to question the lack of justice talk so far. But honestly, to understand justice, I think we must first realize that structured love through shalom does not settle scores, as in "an eye for an eye and a tooth for a tooth," but rather it seeks to alleviate power differentials that continue to create and re-create injustices. In other words, if we understand justice only through the lens of legality, we will simply re-create injustice.

Jesus' proclamation of a "new kingdom" was not to dispense with the legalities of shalom justice but rather to help first-century Palestinians see that love is the ultimate intention of shalom and that justice without the whole picture of shalom is shallow. Shalom was not a new construct to first-century Palestinian Jews under Roman occupation. As I mentioned earlier, we glimpse shalom in Genesis—it is as old as creation and the story of the garden of Eden. Jesus made the shalom kingdom new because he insisted on prioritizing the aspect of love as fulfilling shalom and taught that shalom must have an organic component, not just a structured one. I refer to this as the Spirit *of* shalom, and the Spirit working *in* shalom, which is that organic process of love.

Jesus' insistence on equality, dignity, empowerment, justice, equity, peace, fairness, and similar concepts was based upon the intentionality of shalom's purpose—namely, to bring everything back into God's reconciled shalom community. A shalom community may not be a perfect community but it should be a *just* community. Shalom in ethic and structure is creating true justice as it moves society toward living out these values in love, with one another and even with our enemies. By utilizing postcolonial theologies in deconstructing theologies of empire and developing systems of justice built on shalom, we are able to understand better how to live as postcolonial followers of Jesus.

Putting It to the Test

Bo: How do we test our postcolonial theologies?

Randy: In the introduction, we emphasized *doing* in our paradigm as opposed to *knowledge*. Naturally, in order to test our deconstructive/reconstructive process, we can ask what our new paradigm is doing and how well it is accomplishing the things it does. In other words, is shalom becoming a shared reality among the whole community? But I think there is an even more verifiable test.

Shalom can always be tested on the margins of society. Shalom not only addresses the needs of the most vulnerable, the most disenfranchised, those least able to help themselves, but it also tests our attitudes toward the most marginalized in society. We must always ask ourselves, Are they, the marginalized, being well cared for? Is there both equity (everyone has what is needed) and equality (everyone is as equal as possible)? Are the most downtrodden in the community viewed with inherent dignity by those in power?

Bo: How do you understand the difference between equity and equality? There seems to be a good amount of controversy surrounding these concepts.

Randy: I think equality may be viewed as an issue of justice, meaning, Do all people receive fair treatment? Do we all have the same opportunities? Equity may be seen as an issue of dignity, meaning, Do all people have enough of what is needed to feel the common dignity of humanity? And here they overlap: Do all have the same opportunities to obtain more? I would say that in our modern society equality is most often decided in the courts and equity is most often established through safety nets and creative programs that benefit the poor and marginalized. Currently, one of the dilemmas of our society is that there seem to be two types of justice, one for White folks and another for people of color. Another concern is the diminishing presence of safety nets for the most marginalized in our society. Unfortunately, these concerns are being ignored by the majority of Republicans, and they are supported largely by Evangelicals.

Bo: Because shalom as a community ethos is so very different from the dominant ethos of society today, achieving it can seem almost like an impossibility. That's why I'm asking very practical questions.

Randy: I think that because we have all been so embedded in this strange quagmire of broken theology, patched together here with duct tape and there with baling wire, we are at a place where we are just beginning to understand the difficult reality of the postcolonial task and viewing life through a postcolonial theological lens. We can't forget the obvious truth that Jesus' message of shalom is antithetical to most North American values—and I do seriously mean the polar opposite, especially in our current political climate.

Bo: I want us to be careful here not to alienate some readers, but please expand on those thoughts.

Randy: Shalom, in North American society, would be a reversal of many of the effects of the European invasion and its accompanying philosophical foundation, the European Enlightenment. The Enlightenment was all about the mind.

Descartes: "I think, therefore I am." But *doing* shalom embodies cooperation above competition. *Doing* shalom puts community above the individual. *Doing* shalom recognizes and creates systems of reciprocity with the land and all the community of creation rather than casting creation, including created people, in a utilitarian framework by insisting they must produce for me or increrase my profit margins. Shalom living is also quite keen on diversity.

Heterogeneity, or diversity, is absolutely essential to shalom systems and therefore crucial to postcolonial theologies. The "otherness" of our neighbor is rooted deep within the construct of shalom. By addressing the needs of the other, such as by extending hospitality, we are inherently concerned about the unity to be found in diversity. The United States government has, up until now, operated on the philosophical myth of sameness (homogeneity), privileging and normalizing White, landowning men. God's government operates on different principles. The whole model of Trinitarian structural communal reciprocity demands both unity and diversity, both commonality and difference. God's mission is an exchange of human dignity found through diversity and through relationships of humility. The followers of Jesus are not only *bringing* a message of acceptance to the cultural other, as they live out Jesus' words and example, but they too are being converted to Jesus' truth found *in* the other—even the truth found *in* our enemies, who most often are those who are different from us. I think Creator is often, if not always, using the person we think of or refer to as "the other" to convert *us*.

Bo: There is a lot being said here. I want people to get this. I don't want it to be inaccessible to people.

Randy: And neither do I. As I mentioned early on, almost since its founding, Christianity has been embedded with an imperial theology—a theology of creating injustice for "the other," often resulting in colonization. Therefore, if Christianity is to be associated with the life of Jesus, then colonial forms of Christianity shouldn't be considered Christian. Postcolonial theologies are one of the many theologies that help us separate colonized Christianity from decolonized Christianity—and fortunately for us, postcolonial theologies of decolonization and anticolonization and postcolonial theology proper come in all shapes, sizes, and colors: liberation theologies, womanist theologies, indigenous theologies, ecofeminist theologies, Christian anarchist theologies, etc. These types of theologies, although somewhat different (and each raising our consciousness in a particular area), all intersect somewhere with postcolonial theologies in that they challenge an aspect of empire, or even empire itself. Such theologies help us more accurately reflect the life of Jesus by deconstructing imperial, racist, sexist, and materialistic theologies, and then subsequently reconstructing those theologies based on shalom. In some ways, the term *postcolonial theologies* includes all of these theologies together, since each one holds up important truths to share that flow from understanding a decolonized Jesus.

Did Jesus Intend to Start a Religion?

Bo: Let's talk more about understanding Jesus through a decolonizing lens.

Randy: Clearly, Jesus never commanded his followers to begin a new religion, and as I mentioned earlier, Jesus never became a Christian! Jesus asked those who were Jews to follow him as Jews. He asked Gentiles to follow him as Gentiles. I will say it again: Jesus never became a Christian. He never tried to start another religion. He most often simply said, "Follow me." He never asked anyone to formulate a "sinner's prayer." He mentioned being "born again" just once, but Jesus said "follow me" dozens of times. If Jesus did not intend to start a religion, we might ask ourselves, What kind of movement did Jesus intend to start and what is the role of postcolonial theologies in helping us understand the mission of such a movement?

We have already pointed out the fact that Jesus was fulfilling the mission of shalom because he was a Jew. But what was his context? From a postcolonial perspective, we may understand the mission of Jesus to be one of a local, praxis-oriented theologian living in the Galilee region of Palestine during the era of Second Temple Judaism. Jesus himself used a local community hermeneutic that contained cosmic implications, which included strategizing against empire. Apparently, Jesus understood himself as fulfilling the mission of shalom among his own people (Luke 4:14–21). And he also understood the intent of a more universalized shalom among other people groups, beyond his own local setting (Luke 4:24–27). Postcolonial interests may therefore reject the more Westernized Christ narrative in favor of a more textual and narrative-based historical analysis. Rather than continuing to embrace Christ in the abstract, one point where we can anchor him to reality is within the realm of universal shalom.

An abstract view of Christ simply perpetuates the innate flaw of modern theology, which is to equate knowledge with spirituality. If Jesus is to be interpreted at all, he must be understood as real, concrete, and practical. Jesus is not a metaphor, nor is he simply illustrative. Jesus is not an abstraction simply meant to inspire us. Jesus the man and the spirit of Jesus as Creator, as Christ and as Christ figure among all cultures, are, for the purposes of many postcolonial theologies, inseparable. I would like to argue that Christ, viewed through a postcolonial lens—namely, Jesus as a local, land-based, praxis-oriented, shalom-based theologian possessing a hermeneutic of community—re-indigenizes the story and stories of the gospel. I would add that the Jesus story of history, as a story of good news to all peoples everywhere, is good news to the whole earth. And these stories in all cultures of the Christ figure are inseparably tied into his humanity.

Bo: How do you see our current society in relationship to colonization? I know your experience is different than mine.

Randy: While the era of Christian colonial conversions by force has, I hope, ended—an era that included the Crusades, the Inquisitions, the Doctrine of Discovery, Native American and African American enslavement, Manifest Destiny, Indian residential/boarding schools, Jim Crow, the cult of domesticity, and so on—the ripple effects of colonial theology's devastation, and the purportedly more humane systems of neocolonialism that support the goals of Christian conquest, remain intact. Western Christianity's preoccupation with its own extrinsically categorical worldview within a systemic binary leaves little room for other possibilities. Postcolonial theologies, then, should recognize and repudiate the histories of oppression that disregarded the rights of the others and often failed to recognize the ubiquitous theologically influenced systems that uphold colonialism's theological grip.[3] These

3. Theologically, the modern plight to define Jesus, as evidenced by the "third quest" for the historical Jesus, centers much of the debate concerning the historicity of Jesus and New Testament documents (*à la* The Jesus Seminar) and, taking the text seriously, discussing Jesus' humanity juxtaposed with his divinity (N. T. Wright). We contend that even when one interprets Jesus as an allegory (Spong), it is crucial to take the whole of the allegory seriously. People live according

gies, like the stories of Jesus himself, must lead not
quiescing to empire's unjust and inhumane systems
ʌower, but rather they must lead to speaking truth to
ᵣ wer and dismantling the illegitimate use of power.

Modern explorations in various areas of research have
been helpful to understand the historical Jesus but they seem
to have failed to comprehend the narrative from the local
grounding of the story. This is where Indigenous theology
may be helpful. Theologically, modernity's constructs fail
to comprehend the importance of a more Indigenous approach, one of place-based, shalom mission. Naturally, the
postcolonial theologian should ask how it would even be
possible for Jesus to understand himself outside of his own
local, place-based context, and yet it seems that, to some
degree, he does so by having a very wide lens, including Creator's concern for non-Jews. Re-indigenizing the story and
stories of Jesus through other lenses, such as an Indigenous
worldview, offers an alternative theological perspective that
may be missing from the current scholarship.

Gospel accounts, as seen through the lens of an Indigenous worldview, that intersect both precolonial and
postcolonial worldviews and other postcolonial theologies,
help us understand why it is critical to view the Christ,
who "created the world and everything in it," in a local,
praxis-oriented construct of place. The historical Jesus
looks different through a shalom-based, local, Indigenous,
place-based theological lens. The Indigenous focus on Jesus' relationship to creation, incarnation, life, crucifixion,

---

to their myths. The scientific method fails by deconstructing the history and leaving followers without myth. Again, people live by their
myths. Early Christology studies come much closer to a postcolonial
view than the historical Jesus research because it asks the deeper
questions of the narrative, such as, How did Jesus understand himself? Additionally, each focus has lacked a local, place-based theology, and postcolonial theology must also be about place.

and resurrection is different from a modern Evangelical view. Modern Evangelical views consistently produce a redemption-based replacement theology and replacement missiology[4] that have destroyed, and continue to destroy, many Indigenous cultures. A more Indigenous viewpoint has direct implications for how we lead our lives, how we understand our own salvation/healing, and how we go about doing mission.

Some Postcolonial Theologies

Bo: I know the theological concept of place is important to you and other Indigenous people. Can you say a word about place?

Randy: Theologically, and missiologically, we might begin to think about place by asking in what ways God is already active in our own culture and in the culture of others. To do the will of God we attempt to follow the signs, the leadings of the Spirit, including the obvious and sometimes not so obvious ways that God is already at work, right? Jesus was an example in this realm. Jesus said he did what he saw his father doing. Constant revelation, or what we can call spiritual illumination, was a part of his journey. Jesus' journey was one situated in a particular place. Indigenous theologies could be considered as original creation

4. Missiologist Steven Bevans makes a distinction between a *creation-based* missiology and a *redemption-based* missiology. A redemption-based approach "is characterized by the conviction that culture and human experience are either in need of a radical trans-formation or in need of total replacement" (*Models of Contextual Theology*, 21). According to Bevans, in the redemption-based model, grace replaces creation because creation is corrupt. Most Indigenous peoples do not relate well to a theology that views the creation as evil. Indigenous people have seen the Creator in God's handiwork for far too long to understand it as inherently corrupted.

theologies. Within creation theology is found the idea of a natural process of revelation in a particular place.

> The heavens tell of the glory of God.
>> The skies display his marvelous craftsmanship.
> Day after day they continue to speak;
>> night after night they make him known.
> They speak without a sound or a word;
>> their voice is silent in the skies;
> yet their message has gone out to all the earth,
>> and their words to all the world.
> The sun lives in the heavens where God placed it.
> (Ps 19:1–4 NLT)

> For the truth about God is known to them instinctively. God has put this knowledge in their hearts. From the time the world was created, people have seen the earth and sky and all that God made. They can clearly see his invisible qualities—his eternal power and divine nature. So they have no excuse whatsoever for not knowing God. (Rom 1:19–20 NLT)

One reason that Native Americans and other Indigenous peoples have a history of being banned from self-theologizing is that Western mission models were limited in their understanding of Indigenous culture, worldview, spirituality, and theology. Past mission models were often based on the presupposition that the Indigenous understanding of the Creator and the creation was simplistic and without merit. This misconception may be related to the fact that many of the early missionaries did not believe that God had spoken to Native Americans prior to European arrival or that Native Americans possessed an adequate theology of Christ. Certainly in the Americas, as was the case in other lands invaded by the Europeans, no European assigned much value to or adhered to local Indigenous theology. And yet we find in the Scriptures a constant reference to the created world. We often see Jesus referring to the things found in creation as spiritual inspiration and as models. Rather than merely talk about what Jesus said about creation, Indigenous theologians do what Jesus did: they observe creation and learn from it. There is a quote I like from a Dakota physician who lived in the early twentieth century and who became a Christian:

> Long before I ever heard of Christ, or saw a White man, I had learned from an untutored woman the essence of morality. With the help of dear Nature herself, she taught me things simple but of mighty import. I knew God. I perceived what goodness is. I saw and I loved what is really beautiful. Civilization has not taught me anything better!

—Charles Ohiyesa Eastman (Dakota)[5]

Many Indigenous values include an already present relationship with the Creator. Indigenous peoples see God in creation and learn from creation as a sacred task. This observation turned into understanding and practice is the essence of creation theology. Later, I want to make the case for a particular aspect of theology that includes "the cosmic Christ." I want to link the Jesus of the Scriptures to the Christ revealed in creation and to place. But before I go there, I want to ask you to introduce everyone to a more historical view of theologies of empire and have you provide us with some tools for the journey. So, can I ask you some questions now?

Bo: Ask away!

5. Eastman, *Soul of the Indian*, 29.

2

Colonial Christianity

Randy: I suppose before we frame some important historical constructs we should first talk about historiography, how we understand history.

Bo: When we begin to look at history, and specifically church history, it can be difficult to reconcile some of the unresolved issues that arise without asking challenging questions. It can also be confusing to *double back* on the tradition and story that delivered us to where we are.

If we are Christians asking these questions it can feel as though we are being critical of those who came before us or that we are holding them to our standard and that we somehow know better than they did. It can seem as if we are sawing the very branch of the tree that we are standing on. For these reasons we should ask some very important questions. Would we have done better if we lived in that time? Was there anyone in the era who raised an objection or provided an alternative voice? Is it our place to criticize or critique the tradition?

Randy: Exactly! Some people feel we don't have the right to question our histories.

Bo: As those who follow Jesus, we have both a permission and precedent given to us in the example of Jesus. Jesus did not settle for the status quo. Jesus did not accept the way things were as the way they would always be—or the way God wanted them to be. Jesus told stories and asked questions that called into question the assumed order of things and the authority by which they had come to be that way.

Jesus' approach questioned deeply the way that things seemed. He undermined and subverted the established order and institutional assumption of his day. He bucked the powers and the systems that were in operation. Jesus both modeled and called for *a way* of being in the world that exposed *truth* and nourished *life*. Christians, then, following Jesus' (and Paul's) example, have both permission and precedent for examining assumptions, systems, and histories through what we can call a *christological lens*. Through this lens we may ask questions such as, Does this idea sound like the sort of thing Jesus supported? Does this way of doing things conform to the example provided by Jesus? Does this system lead to treating people the way that Jesus treated people?

Randy: Are we back to talking about power?

Bo: One of the unavoidable realities that looking at church history is going to bring to the surface is the issue of control through the illegitimate use of power. Many times, church history is presented as the history of ideas and doctrines. Other times it appears as important figures that are highlighted and given focus. While these two approaches have merit, they are not the entire story or even the most significant elements of the story.

Authority has often manifested itself historically through the illegitimate use of power—attempting to control others, even through violence. These are understandably unpleasant elements of the past that many would rather avoid. Exposing violence and other means of control, however, is unavoidable if one is utilizing a christological lens. This is true not only because of what Jesus said and did but also because of Jesus' own story and history. Jesus was killed by the authorities because he could not be controlled, because he was a threat to the established order. We must enter into any examination of history with sober and sincere humility and ask, How did things come to be this way? And what do we do with the elements that don't seem to line up with Jesus' life and message? Respectfully, we take up the permission and precedent that is provided to us in Christ.

Digging Deeper

Randy: How do postcolonial approaches critique history?

Bo: Entering into a postcolonial approach, and given my location that is specifically anticolonial, provides us with some new tools and concepts for our exploration. Two examples come in the form of *a hermeneutic of suspicion* and *critical theory*. A hermeneutic of suspicion is not as negative as it may sound initially. In fact, it can be very constructive and liberating to *ask the question behind the question*! Hermeneutics simply means "a way of interpreting," and a hermeneutic of suspicion basically asks questions like the following:

- How did we come to know this?
- Who was doing the reporting?
- Who made the decisions about the report?

- Who, if anyone, was excluded?

- Is anyone's voice or perspective missing?

- Why are certain voices missing?

- Who policed the conversation?

- How was the policing enforced?

These and other questions are a way of investigating the past that both acknowledges the *beliefs* and *key figures* as they have traditionally come to us and allows us to explore the underlying systems of power that were operating at a lower register.

Randy: Sounds good so far. Can you give an example?

Bo: Music provides a great analogy for talking about different registers. When people talk about a song they often focus on the lyrics or words. They may even say that the lyrics are what the song is *about*. Others may go further and analyze the melody, the harmony, or the bass line. All of those critiques are operating on different registers, and when they come together they form what gets categorized as *the music*. It is interesting to note that even though the words may get the lion's share of attention, if you took away the lyrics you would still have a song.[1] If someone is really into music they may examine the tempo, rhythm, timbre, pitch, and instrumentation. All of this falls within analyzing the music. The only thing that might seem objectionable is if somebody says, "Stop pulling it apart and just let me listen to the song!"

In our music analogy, where things get tricky is when someone begins to ask questions about what is going on

1. Stated beliefs and doctrines may function the same way in Christian history and organizations—but that is a conversation for a different time.

behind the scenes. Why was this artist selected and not another? Did this person write their own song or was it provided for them? How much money was spent on production and promotion with this artist? Did the record label pay for this song to be played in prime rotation slots or for the artist to be featured in media campaigns?

In a similar way, critical theory provides us a net to catch all of the unaccounted-for details and the unresolved loose ends. Critical theory challenges us not to absorb or assume the highlights of a story without addressing the lowlights as well. That is the danger of history, after all—because history is said to be written by the victors, it is often re-presented as a glory tale. Critical theory makes sure that the highlight reel doesn't *whitewash* the uglier parts of the story—it does this by accounting for the messy, or less flattering, aspects of the story.

Critical theory introduces a concept called *negative dialectics* that requires us to look at both the positives and the negatives of society's historical road. We can concede that history is indeed moving forward, but also acknowledge that it is not always in a straight line, nor is it always a smooth ride. In fact, the road of history is often a bumpy ride, even for those on *top,* but we must especially take stock of the many who get run over by the machine and end up on the *underside* of "progress."

Because the historical age known as "the Enlightenment" or "age of reason" created such a change of principles and values in Western societies, and contributes even in the formation of our current discussion, we should ask a few critical questions:

- The Enlightenment brought "light" to many aspects of society. What was the dark side?

- The "age of reason" had many advantages and advancements. What do we do with the unreasonable elements like genocide and slavery?

- Western civilization had a mission to *civilize* foreign peoples. What about the uncivilized tactics of those who carried out that mission?

- How do we process the un-Christlike behavior of those who attempted to convert Indigenous and other peoples to Christ by threat of the sword (or by the lynching tree)?

Randy: Okay, it's becoming clearer, but how about another example for those of us, like me, who learn more by example than theory?

Bo: Here's another analogy. If you think about a story (or history) as a math formula, then facts, dates, and names are often presented in the same manner as givens, variables, and outcomes or solutions. Negative dialects is interested in the *leftovers* or *remainders*. What do they tell us about the equation as it has been presented to us? More importantly, do the leftovers, the left-outs, and the remainders change the equation in a way that makes it merely inaccurate or ultimately untrue?

These two sets of tools provide us with a hermeneutic of suspicion and a negative dialectic that allows us to adjust our christological lens and begin to look at both the way things are and the way that they came to be. We use Jesus' permission and precedent to interrogate (question) the current system and challenge the status quo. We want to examine the operative register of control and power in order to explore the way things could be and imagine the world (and the church) working a different way.

Categorizing Imperial Theologies

Randy: What do postcolonial concerns do for us when theologizing?

Bo: Postcolonial concerns are not necessarily (or even primarily) focused on history and the past. Many have as their main emphasis the concrete, lived reality of everyday people and modern communities. However, when addressing issues of the past, one might begin asking a different set of questions, such as these:

- We know from history what ended up being in the various creeds of the church—but who made up the councils that formulated and voted on the creeds?
- How did one get invited to the council?
- How was the council funded?
- How did one come to be a bishop?
- Who policed the conversation?
- Was there any dissension or disagreement?
- What happened to dissenters?
- Were there any voices not present?

Colonial or imperial theologians were those who failed to challenge the authority of empire—for example, Augustine, theologian to the Constantinian empire; Aquinas and Erasmus, theologians to the Roman Catholic empire; and Luther and Calvin, theologians to the Protestant empires of Europe. Where they challenged empire on its authority to exert control, they were doing postcolonial theology, but, on the other hand, none of them was consistent enough in his overall theology to be called a postcolonial theologian.

Most of them were, regretfully, theologians who supported empire of some type.

Randy: Help us understand more about how these venerated theologies can be understood.

Adding a Modifier

Bo: One of the fascinating trends in the past fifty years is the tendency to splinter and label different perspectives and emphases with modifiers. This has happened in medicine with the trend to specialize—from being a doctor to being a general practitioner, and the subsequent division into specialists such as podiatrists, pediatricians, optometrists, OB/GYNs, proctologists, urologists, and oncologists. This same thing has happened in the music industry, where styles have been formalized into distinct genres of classical, folk, country, western, jazz, soul, gospel, R&B, blues, CCM, rock, alternative, indie rock, classic rock, heavy metal, punk, grunge, etc. Each of these categories gets parsed further into subcategories—within classical, for instance, subcategories include chamber music, orchestral, strings, opera, and symphony.

While the above list of medical doctors and musical genres may be interesting, the implication of this trend when it comes to theological perspectives is concerning. These may be helpful specializations within other fields, but this tendency has had a debilitating effect in theology. Unlike other areas, the designation *music* does not confer the unspoken label of "real" and anything with a modifier becomes "less than." Unfortunately, in theological circles, traditional or classic approaches get to be theology proper and everything else is required to qualify itself as if it were a junior member and had to earn its seat at the table.

Postcolonial concerns, however, have a different way of looking at this historical development. In the new landscape, no one gets to claim a privileged place on tradition or legacy alone. Everyone gets modified and everyone has to explain what their project is all about. There are no free passes and no one gets to be "regular" or "normal." We are all up to something, and we each take our turn qualifying our project and justifying our approach. Postcolonial theologies are a convention of peers and a conference of equals.

Applying critical theory has an amazing capacity to level the playing field and expose what have been historical privileges and unexamined advantages. Each school of thought and tradition comes to the arena and puts its best foot forward. It explains its priorities, its goals, its big questions and major concerns. Each one gets to frame its project with its own categories, vocabulary, and concepts. This way no one has a home-field advantage (to use a sports analogy). Then the examination begins. The question then becomes, What is your relationship to the powers and authorities?

Can you imagine what would happen if no theology got a free pass and came to be thought of as "normal" or "regular" or "standard"? *What if we started calling standard, unmodified theology chauvinist theology, or white theology?* What would get exposed? What would be the implications? What if we had to classify theologies that came through Europe as *consumerist,* or *colonial,* or *Greco-Roman*? The reality is that this is not a theoretical exercise—this process is currently underway in postcolonial, contextual, feminist, and many other circles.

The above italicized text is from an essay by Brian McLaren. He continues by saying,

> The covert assumption behind the modifier post-colonial thus becomes overt, although it is generally more obliquely and politely stated

> than this: Standard, normative, historic, so-
> called orthodox Christian theology has been a
> theology of empire, a theology of colonialism,
> a theology that powerful people used as a tool
> to achieve and defend land theft, exploitation,
> domination, superiority, and privilege.[2]

Randy: Sounds very much like postcolonial theologies can achieve the kind of shalom systems I mentioned earlier.

Bo: The impact of this shift cannot be overstated. Gone are the days of the overconfident, triumphalist swagger that unapologetically swings the past like a bat and assumes that the way things are is just the way God wants them to be. There is a growing historical consciousness that wants to slow things down and take a closer look before one (too confidently) proclaims a *theologia gloriae*. What is evident is a newer tone of humility and caution, with less chest-thumping and trumpeting the glorious past. Many theologians agree that we have good news for the world and that there is a gospel of hope to proclaim; it is just tempered and buffered by a level of awareness that has not always been present in our march to glory.

Reality Setting In

Randy: Maybe more humility is what was needed all along?

Bo: Awareness and humility are evident across the board—from new postmodern movements like the emergent church conversation, missional approaches, neomonastic communities, etc., and even into traditional denominations and

2. McClaren, "Post-Colonial Theology," lines 9–13.

missions agencies.[3] Of course, not all groups have awakened to this new reality, nor has humility and self-awareness equally caught on across the theological spectrum. There are even groups that are retrenching and defensively doubling down, but they are doing so in response to a radically altered atmosphere and a rapidly changing landscape. The rules of the game have changed.

One of the significant shifts that can be seen in the culture of many organizations and groups is the move away from paternalistic and hierarchical models and metaphors (word pictures) to more communal and participatory ones. A cynic may say that these changes are nothing more than verbiage or semantics, but I want to argue that this is a sign of a much larger concern that is undermining the assumptions of the past and the blind acceptance of *the way things are*. Even the way we talk about mission, mutuality, and partnership is an acknowledgment that the colonial missions approach was flawed, at best, and warped at worst.

Randy: How so?

Bo: Analogies, word pictures, and framing metaphors are telling. Jesus used a lot of farming analogies, and colonial missions continued to use agrarian word pictures even as history moved into a more industrial age. The imagination of colonial missions was fertilized by the idea of the "seed of the gospel." Part of the driving mission of the colonial impulse was to transplant this seed (or seedling) of the gospel into foreign soil. The powerful assumption behind this impulse was that missionaries had "the truth" and

3. You can see this in everything from recruitment strategies, fund-raising difficulties, concerns about diversity in leadership, and numerous other areas that come together to form a new configuration of priorities, sometimes within the organization and other times merely in its response to the surrounding constituency.

simply needed to transport and impose that (European) understanding of the gospel into a different context, where it would take root and, inevitably, take on a life of its own.

This approach, it turns out, had some unforeseen side effects and consequences due to its unexamined assumptions and unaccounted-for relationships to power. The ugly legacy of colonial missions is that it piggybacked on the economic and governmental mechanisms of colonialism and in so doing provided a level of validation and sanctification for domination and exploitation of foreign peoples and lands. This is an aspect of Christian history that many people would like to ignore, if not conceal. Unfortunately, it was not only the way the gospel got here but was largely the message itself.[4] Western "civilization" and its cultural expectations were imported and imposed on Indigenous peoples in an odd amalgamation of church and state, form and content, message and delivery.

Randy: How do you understand this colonial impulse of Christianity?

Bo: The reality is that the marriage of mission and colonial power/violence has marred the purity of the missionary impulse and corrupted the mechanism of denominational leadership and oversight. Yes, the gospel message benefited in one sense from being tucked into the economic and governmental enterprises of the colonial era. In another sense, it compromised its very message of the *way of Jesus* by marrying the vessels of power that carried it across the oceans and planted it on foreign shores. The era traded the simple purity of its message for a political expediency and unearned promotion that ultimately compromised its very message and called into question the entire enterprise.

4. Even if this message of subjugation and domination was an unintended consequence.

This deeply flawed paradigm is why postcolonial conversations are so vital. They ask the question behind the question:

- We know what happened—but *why* did it happen?
- We see the way things are—but *how* did they come to be this way?
- We see the results—but *what* was the cost?
- We can study history—but *who* is telling that history?
- We know that there were victims—but *when* do we hear from the victims?
- We admit that there may be a need for repentance, reconciliation, and reparations—but *where* would that happen?

Like a shark in a swimming pool, there is little that can remain the same once the questions of postcolonial theologies are in the water. When postcolonial concerns are introduced to the conversation, the entire enterprise is called into question. Once a postcolonial approach takes an active posture, we can no longer hide behind success or legacy, history or tradition, authority or power. One must account for the *ways* in which this scope of ministry came to be. Not only have the rules of the game changed, but the very ways in which we measure "success" are being called into question.

Direction and Location

Randy: How do Jesus' clear teachings and humble life example get wrapped in the theologies of empire?

Bo: Colonial mentalities are notoriously dualistic. Dualism occurs not simply when there seems to be a pair of options but when those options are presented as (1) a binary and as (2) oppositional or adversarial. Some examples are Christian and pagan, civilized and savage, modern and primitive, science and superstition, natural and unnatural, man and beast, mind and body, lost and saved. This tendency is difficult to break, as so many of our inherited categories are framed within this convenient packaging system. Remnants of it linger in the postcolonial approach with its focus on center and margin.

Postcolonial approaches are concerned not only with *where* an author-thinker-practitioner is located but also with the direction in which they are moving.[5] Within the postcolonial conversation is a unique collection of concerns and emphases. These include the decolonial, anticolonial, and postcolonial in overlapping and expanding circles of emphasis. These are not limiting and adversarial categories but are concerned with the situated nature of knowledge and the intended audience/purpose.

Randy: Address location and direction—or, as I have heard you ask, "Is the author or speaker located at the center or the margin and is her concern those at the center or the margin?"

Bo: Let me use the two of us as an example. We, the current authors, have differing locations. I'll use our proper names for the reader's benefit. If Randy is speaking as a Native follower of Jesus and his concern is for Native issues, that is a different enterprise than if Bo is writing as a White Christian and his concern is the ongoing systems of power that continue to marginalize and oppress Native American communities. If Randy is writing as a Native Jesus follower to White Christians who are at the center of power about

5. This line of thought comes from Jewish liberation theologian Marc Ellis. His books *Practicing Exile*, *Toward a Jewish Liberation Theology*, and *Future of the Prophetic* are profound.

how their beliefs and policies have marginalized Native peoples, you have a third aspect to the approach. These are not entirely different conversations, and they can be mutually informing and mutually beneficial. Both location and direction matter here. The desire is not to parse and label in order to discount and disqualify but instead to get away from the abstract and *objective* notion of "truth" that has plagued the Western mind.

Postcolonial approaches recognize both that knowledge is radically situated and that meaning is contested. No one has all the truth. No one has a God's-eye perspective. No one stands outside of their experience. No one is wholly objective. We speak as subjects and our perspective is subjective. This is where the postcolonial approach and the postmodern one have some overlap. Information is seen to be partial, provisional, and perspectival: partial because knowledge is not encyclopedic and totalizing; provisional because knowledge is not always fixed and permanent, but temporary and reversible; perspectival because knowledge is socially located and mediated.

Another way to say this is that meaning is constructed or negotiated. Meaning does not happen in a vacuum, nor is it abstract. It is located within a context and is thus both situated and negotiated. Within this understanding, both location and direction matter, and one way of addressing that is by understanding the decolonial and anticolonial emphases. Anticolonial emphasis comes from centers of power, and both the perspective and the approach is inseparably linked to those constructs and frameworks. Decolonial thought, on the other hand, comes from the margins and may employ anticolonial approaches in an effort to achieve its results. The two may engage in similar tactics or employ identical methods, but by the very nature of their positioning, they are not doing (entirely) the same thing. They may say the same thing at points, but they are not speaking with the same voice.[6]

Decolonial is not simply a set of concerns but a *located-ness* that is unique and particular within the conversation. This delineation is no binary or dualistic categorization, for they are not mutually excluding. It results from recognition of one's identity within the colonial project and the resulting possibility to speak and act *from* a place *in* a direction. Don't be embarrassed, Randy, but I'm going to quote you now.

> Among the many things I have been realizing over the past few years is the extent to which we Indians have to get un-brainwashed. Unlike some situations where the gospel was presented without strong colonial constraints, we must not only contextualize the gospel to our own culture, but we must first go through the painful process of de-colonization.[7]

Decolonial voices such as Che Guevara, Aimé Césaire, Frantz Fanon, and you yourself (to name a few) are vital to contend with, and while they may agree with historically anticolonial perspectives (Las Casas, Jesuits, and Lenin), their location and direction give them a very different and meaningful distinction. Though they may comment on the same issues or hold the same opinions on those issues, there is a significant distinction in the location from which the critique is drawn and the direction in which it is pointed.

6. This distinction is important because while Bo is anticolonial, he speaks from the center. He does not come from a community that has been marginalized or colonized. Randy speaks to decolonize and he is also anticolonial. Randy has the ability to do that—Bo does not. Postcolonial conversation makes this distinction, and it highlights the importance of Native perspectives over those that have been historically privileged. This delineation comes from Bo's time of studying with Santiago Slabodsky.

7. Woodley, *When Going to Church Is Sin*, 141.

A concern has arisen as to the possibility of someone from the center having the ability to bring a substantial critique. Can one level a valid critique on the program as a whole? Is it possible to review one's location and particular constructs to the degree that a valid attempt might be made at a critique for the enterprise one is socialized in? It is possible as long as one acknowledges a core reality: anticolonialism is housed within colonial frameworks and is inherently (genetically) of the same material. Anticolonial thought is therefore cancerous to its host organism. Though it is comprised of the same genetic material and from the same biological makeup, it operates in such a way as to undermine the colonial project and subvert the enterprise altogether.

Social Imaginaries

Randy: Then how does one within the system begin?

Bo: Those engaged in anticolonial projects can find it challenging to break free from inherited philosophical frameworks that are deeply entrenched in and central to Western thought. Some find an ally in more recent forms of philosophical thought within the likes of poststructuralism and postmodern or continental approaches. An example of this cross-pollination is the concept of "social imaginaries" found in the work of Charles Taylor and Benedict Anderson.

Social imaginaries are larger and more formal versions of devices and constructs that we use commonly in everyday conversation. They can be a helpful way to picture (mental maps) and designate, sort, and categorize the world of experience in order to help it make sense. Mental constructs can serve as placeholders, such as when politicians speak of "the American people" or "the people of Florida." No politician has met or surveyed every American or Floridian, so lumping them together is between a stretch and a form of misplaced concreteness. Mental constructs are a constant presence in modern society, but they become pronounced in election cycles. Politicians and reporters use them to bunch and generalize groups for convenience. We hear about soccer moms, the evangelical vote, the Latino community, Black voters—as if everyone in that group can be assumed to be homogenous and the grouping spoken of as a unit.

Benedict Anderson in *Imagined Communities* and Charles Taylor in *Modern Social Imaginaries* both utilize the concept of social imaginaries to examine the past and address the present. Taylor breaks it down into three parts: first, social imaginaries are a way that people commonly imagine themselves and their connection to the larger group. Second, it refers to a way that this imaginary is portrayed and imparted in narratives, songs, myths, and ceremony. Third, it addresses the ways that this conception is enacted and embodied in physical or concrete ways in order to establish and reinforce the narrative. Taylor uses the analogy of a three-legged stool in which the presence of all three elements provide stability to the identity of the individual and the group. Mental constructs such as "Canadian" are reinforced by songs (national anthems), rituals (hockey night), and stories (role in the global community). The third supporting leg is when standard mental constructs are elevated into social imaginaries.

Social imaginaries have historically been present in every group and in every era. These mental constructs are designed to allow for clarity in thought and ease of classification while facilitating a kind of shortcut in communicating. However, they have taken on exponential importance in the last three centuries as monarchal rule has given way to the nation-state and late capitalism has morphed into a global market where multinational corporations market their goods to transnational consumers with multicultural images broadcast on multiple media platforms. Issues related to identity, belonging, and community are increasingly fluid as the long-established boundaries and markers are undermined and called into question. Social imaginaries were severely solidified in the middle of the twentieth-century context of World War II and the subsequent Cold War era. Nationality, ethnicity, race, gender, and sexuality all had the appearance of a certainty that was consequential and continues to pose ongoing challenges in the twenty-first century. The question for the contemporary situation is, Who do you mean when you say "us"?

In *Modern Social Imaginaries*, Taylor provides an illustration of a possible anticolonial resource. He details how people(s) "imagine" themselves through "images, stories, and legends."[8] He interposes concepts, time and space with engagements of Marxist thought under *the specter of idealism* as he addresses the societal clashes of colonialism where "the raw meet the cooked." He says,

> Behind the issue of inequality and justice lies something deeper, which touches what today we would call the "identity" of the human beings in those earlier societies. Because their most important actions were the doings of whole groups (tribe, clan, subtribe, lineage), articulated in a certain way . . . they couldn't conceive themselves as potentially disconnected from this social matrix. It would probably never even occur to them to try.[9]

8. Taylor, *Modern Social Imaginaries*, 23.
9. Taylor, *Modern Social Imaginaries*, 54.

The social imaginary provides a framework to examine and critique both the external manifestations and the internal mechanism that drove the colonial machine. Taylor takes on the "story (or myth) of progress" and its significance to modernity. There is a critique of its heady nature and awareness of its dreadful manifestations, but in the end, the real value is found in its capacity to outline the mental furniture and map the conceptual architecture that justified or validated colonial projects and allows them to continue on in neocolonial forms. Taylor acknowledges the problematic European model of socially imagined identities and hopes that "the multiform world . . . will emerge in order and peace. Then the real positive work, of building mutual understanding, can begin."[10]

Terry Eagleton comes under much the same umbrella as one who has scathing criticism of the colonial project and great sympathy for the postcolonial concerns. His concern sounds distinctly anticolonial when he says, "Most of the new theorists were not only 'post' colonialism, but 'post' the revolutionary impetus which had given birth to the new nations in the first place."[11] This concern is within a similar framework to Taylor in their address of identity and the formulations of communal framing of identity:

> Something of the same fate afflicted many of those nations who managed in the twentieth century to free themselves from Western colonial rule. In a tragic irony, socialism proved least possible where it was most necessary. Indeed, postcolonial theory first emerged in the wake of the failure of Third World nations to go it alone. It marked the end of the era of Third World

10. Taylor, *Modern Social Imaginaries*, 196.
11. Eagleton, *After Theory*, Kindle locs. 126–28.

revolutions, and the first glimmerings of what we now know as globalization.[12]

The insights of both Taylor and Eagleton are good; the similarities are clear and the critique is at times palpable. They are potentially valuable to someone engaged in anticolonial concerns.

Decolonial Concerns

Randy: This is really helpful, but to be more concise, in what ways is the decolonial voice different from the anticolonial voice?

Bo: The decolonial voice is different in both the place it speaks *from* and the direction it speaks *to*. When Native American authors like yourself, Taiaiake Alfred, Vine Deloria Jr., Winona LaDuke, George Tinker, and John Mohawk address colonialism, they may at times have great difference between them. That diversity may be accentuated if they engage in European/Western constructs or even those engagements blurred with anticolonial thought that sound similar. What distinguishes them is their location within colonialism and their constitutive non-Western epistemology.

Does a decolonial thinker betray his or her core integrity if the forms employed are inherited from colonial/Western origins? If one writes in English, uses Christian frameworks, participates in academic discourse, or borrows from inherently European ideals, does that taint the author's project and corrupt any possible impact their work might seek to influence? Is it conceivable to utilize the oppressor's forms without reinforcing the very structures that one is attempting to combat and counteract?

12. Eagleton, *After Theory*, Kindle locs. 110–13.

Randy: Or can one use the master's tools to dismantle the master's house?

Bo: That's the question. Our working assumption is that one groomed and formed by the "center" (colonial power) can never fully escape the thought structures and frameworks that give rise to even the most benevolent of concerns. The anticolonial address is directed from the center, infused with power and privilege no matter the individual's particular location within that structure. The decolonial concern is born and subsequently formed within a community and framework that operates with indigenous constructs, myths, language, and rituals.

The importance of this clarification is the *essential complexity* of the contemporary situation. The nature of our interconnected world and the validation of its educational systems pose intense challenges for articulating and distributing a decolonial message outside the frameworks of colonial domination. It is too simple to call these thinkers hybrids or to classify them as intercultural or characterize them as navigators between worlds. The postcolonial landscape is viciously interrelated and complex. Systems, structures, and institutions are so enmeshed in assumption and cooperation that a truly Indigenous voice may never be heard or even have the possibility to surface in any impactful way into this conversation that is layers deep in systemic control.

The Empire and Colonialism

> When the Western world accepted Christianity, Caesar conquered; and the received text of Western theology was edited by his lawyers. . . . The brief Galilean vision of humility flickered throughout the ages, uncertainly. . . . But

the deeper idolatry, of the fashioning of God in the image of the Egyptian, Persian, and Roman imperial rulers, was retained. The Church gave unto God the attributes which belonged exclusively to Caesar.

—Alfred North Whitehead[13]

Randy: That's a great quote. What does it mean to you?

Bo: Okay, let me explain. One tricky aspect of the postcolonial biblical or theological conversation is the uneven translation and historical transition between an imperial impulse and its later colonial form. The two are intrinsically connected while not being exactly identical. The distinction between the earlier imperial structures and the Hebrew and Christian Scriptures would have been contending with the more recent colonial forms of the past couple of centuries and are more a matter of degree than of kind.

The distinction between empire (and the imperial form) with more recent colonial developments, provide a continuity that allows students of the Bible and biblical scholars to be in conversation with postcolonial concerns, whether anti-imperial or decolonial. Empires use military, economic, and governmental means to expand their territory and exert control over conquered populations. Colonial powers utilize these forms of domination and control to establish outposts in faraway lands as virtual extensions of the

13. Whitehead continues, "There is . . . in the Galilean origin of Christianity, yet another suggestion which does not fit in very well. . . . It does not emphasize the ruling Caesar, or the ruthless moralist, or the unmoved mover. It dwells upon the tender elements in the world, which slowly and in quietness operate by love, and it finds purpose in the present immediacy of a kingdom not of this world. Love neither rules, nor is it unmoved; also it is a little oblivious as to morals. It does not look to the future; for it finds its own reward in the immediate present" (*Process and Reality*, 342–43).

foreign empire. Neocolonialism is the continuation of these mechanisms of influence by different means after the demise of almost all formal colonial relationships. The imperial-colonial impulse is still exerting itself in less formalized or official ways, though the underlying mechanisms of power and control are operative through multinational corporations and paramilitary organizations. Maybe we can address neocolonialism more in the final chapter.[14]

The primary question for us here then is, What is your relationship to power? In what way does your community or tradition relate to the operative systems that dominate? Does your group or your leaders take a stand on these historic issues? Has your community or denomination benefited from its relationship to imperial and colonial powers? Have the heroes of your tradition spoken about issues of oppression and marginalization? Has there been a posture of turning a blind eye?

These difficult questions are part of the postcolonial program. Anticolonial and decolonial voices enter into an examination of history with a critical eye in order to inform the postcolonial conversation. Christians have an important role to play in that discourse because of how the gospel has so often been co-opted by the powers that be to pacify the population and baptize the imperial forms. Often in Evangelicalism, and elsewhere, the name of Jesus has throughout history been reduced to a mascot—the cross becoming a hood ornament on the machine of empire. Fortunately, there is vibrant conversation beginning to emerge as voices from historically marginalized communities are brought into conversation with those that have been traditionally privileged.

14. The term *neocolonialism* is thought to have been coined by Ghanaian president Kwame Nkrumah in 1963.

Randy: How do people hear these kinds of voices?

Bo: This is where the difficult and vital work of our task begins. Listening to Indigenous voices and other marginalized perspectives is a great first step. Simply listening might even have a stand-alone value and be a reward on its own! In our culture of homogenized media and sanitized religious gatherings, we might even be tempted to pat ourselves on the back for simply hearing from diverse voices. This is why the postcolonial conversation is so important to the future of the church. We need to both appreciate and engage leaders and thinkers who are involved in decolonial work, but it is not enough to let them shoulder the burden on their own. Those who occupy a place in centers of power must join in the anticolonial task of examining institutional practices, challenging hurtful and oppressive structures, and interrogating narratives of exclusion and superiority.

We need each other for this task. Feeling bad or being upset is not enough. The good news of Jesus Christ is that there is hope for the poor, healing for the wounded, and freedom for the prisoner. When we deal honestly with economic legacies of exploitation and inequality, we participate in the gospel. When we expose historic injuries and work toward restoring shalom between communities, we proclaim the gospel. When we undermine systems of harm and work to subvert operative structures that handcuff communities to institutional despair, we bear witness to the healing work of Christ.

Randy: What bearing do you think Evangelical Christianity's past has on our theological task today?

Bo: History asks each generation particular questions. I believe the question for Western Christians in the twenty-first century is an old and familiar one: Who is my neighbor?

Within the context of this hyper-connected global village, the question *who is my neighbor?* becomes a little easier to answer. The answer is: nearly everyone is our neighbor. We are so interrelated, mutually dependent, and our lives are so interlaced in a web of relationships that it is nearly impossible to close our eyes and not see the need and the hurt of those around the corner or on the other side of the world. We have unprecedented access to communities and voices from every corner of the globe. Answering the question *who is my neighbor?* has never been easier—but owning up to the reality and the implications of our heightened proximity is exponentially more challenging.

Between Google, Twitter, and YouTube any one of us has nearly unlimited access to any information or perspective we could possibly want. Many in our culture feel overwhelmed by this saturation of stimulation and complain of being over-communicated. There is a deadening malaise and compassion fatigue that actually numbs the senses and hardens the heart. This should sound an alarm in the mind of Jesus followers and provide a wake-up call to the community of Christ. Unfortunately, the nature of hegemony means that we unwittingly get conscripted into stories that pacify us, and we can easily be seduced by unceasing and unsatisfying consumerism. Cornel West famously warns against empire's offering of what he terms "weapons of mass distraction" and exhorts us not to become "well-adjusted to injustice and well-adapted to indifference."[15]

Randy: I love that quote.

Bo: Power over others (hegemony) provides those ideas and explanations that we may not even be aware of but that

15. West, *Brother West*, 100.

help us as a society to accept the way things are. Hegemonic narratives are the lifeblood of the empire, convincing good citizens to passively participate in unjust and oppressive economic, legal, and religious systems without asking *the question behind the question.* The unexamined is the enemy of the awakened soul. From birth we are conditioned, groomed, and socialized to think, speak, and act in certain ways. It seems like the most natural thing in the world until we awaken to the fact that not everyone's experience of being human has been the same as ours. We are confronted with a set of questions: Why is that the case? Is that an accident of birth? Is that God's will? Is there something I can do with what I have?

Postcolonial perspectives on belief and faith take this initial awakening and expand it beyond the individual. Access to resources and influence begins to add a weight of responsibility as one realizes the consequential nature of one's participation in the world. The place that we occupy and the power that we have within our networks are important avenues of access and influence. We awaken from our soul-slumber of passivity and self-satisfaction to the harsh reality of colonial legacies as they relate to contemporary issues of race, land, laws, and even religious conflict. The world begins to look very different—behold, if anyone is in Christ, it is as if the whole world looks new to them.

Randy: What does one do with this awakened sense of history and perspective?

Bo: One place to start might be to look at the groups, denominations, and conversations in which you participate. This can be a daunting endeavor. In the past decade I have entered into this postcolonial approach, and so I'll tell you about three groups that I am a part of or in dialogue with as an exercise that, I hope, will be illustrative of the larger issue that can be exposed in a postcolonial analysis. The three groups that will serve to demonstrate different approaches are the emergent church, the missional church, and neomonastic communities.

Three Conversations

The emergent church conversation was a vibrant and dynamic set of conferences, new-church starts, innovative worship expressions, media platforms, and theological engagements. For those of us who are a part of it, the window from 2005 to 2015 was an exhilarating time of spiritual exploration, diverse exchanges online, exciting regional meetings, and ecclesiastic innovation. There is so much that happened and so much that could be reported about this lively moment of post-evangelicals, mainliners, and progressive types coming together in a big-tent approach to Christianity.

People came to the emergent conversation with all their hopes, angst, dreams, woundedness, inspiration, agitation, creativity, and institutional disillusionment. A lot happened in that decade-long window, but perhaps the most telling moment came at the 2010 Emergent Village Theological Conversation. There occurred a time of postcolonial engagement with Musa Dube of Botswana and your good friend, Lakota Sioux author Richard Twiss. It was the moment the conversation attempted to round the corner from innovating worship expression and theological exploration toward issues of power and privilege. People had been asking for an engagement like this with the full realization that it was not sufficient simply to integrate ancient worship practices into contemporary expressions or to infuse our theology with postmodern philosophical concepts if we were not going to deal with larger meta-issues of systemic racism and the colonial legacy.

Afterward, this buildup, the sessions, and the take-aways were discussed on numerous occasions. The sense many participants had at the moment, which has only grown deeper over time, is that of all the emergent events, this one was somewhere between the low point and a rare dud. There was just a sense that something was off or that it was too forced. Some blamed it on the event's being held in conjunction with another massive conference on religion (American Academy of Religion), thus dividing people's time and attention. Others focused on different aspects that all contributed to the surprising disappointment.

In the years that followed we have continued to de-brief with folks who were a part of those meetings and that conversation. The emergent church conversation has lost steam and remains only as a handful of congregations and worship communities scattered around the country. Issues of organization, leadership, diversity, and power might have played a part in this loss of steam. Regardless, the emergent church conversation provided a valuable lesson and an on-going challenge: it is no longer enough to innovate worship expressions and update theological frameworks. Postcolonial concerns about marginalized communities, relationships to forms of power, and issues of leadership and organization must be accounted for and addressed from the outset— otherwise, imperial and colonial mentalities are so ubiqui-tous that they will seep in and be operative by default.

Missional theology has gained quite a bit of traction in some sizable quarters of the Protestant family. Missional thought bridges Evangelical, conservative, charismatic, and even some reformed circles. Missional approaches place an emphasis on the *missional nature* of the gospel—that God came to us. The *missio Dei* teaches us that in both the Hebrew and Christian Testaments, God initiates, closes the gap and finds the people. This tenet is thought to be essential to the nature and character of God. The assumption, then, is that we, as the people of God, must be a *going* people. Missional thought emphasizes *sent-ness* as the nature of the church. That the church is sent is not just essential to its purpose, it is what defines its very purpose: to go and preach the good news of God's love in Jesus' name.

I suppose missional approaches have some resonance for us as authors. I was originally ordained with the Christian & Missionary Alliance. You have been employed as a missionary in the past with the American Baptists and you are academically trained as a missiologist. There are substantial issues that remain, however, related to direction, hierarchy, and paternalism in missional mentalities. The heart and the willingness behind *going* are to be applauded. Jesus modeled an incarnational gospel and contextual approaches are to be valued over attractional models like those found in the megachurch movement. Concerns abound, though, in the shadow of the colonial legacy. How does one reclaim or reform a concept that has been so thoroughly corrupted and has taken on so much baggage? Is repentance enough? Can the form actually be redeemed and repurposed?

Postcolonial awareness requires us to ask questions behind the question: In what *way* is one sent? Does one go with all the answers? Is there an invitation from the receiving community? Is there any mutuality or are the content and form already predetermined by the one going? Are decisions made in a top-down hierarchical manner? Are decisions made unilaterally? Are decisions accountable to the community present or are they reviewed by the sending agency?

The nature and love of God's coming to us is a beautiful thing. The incarnational nature of the gospel of Christ is the heart of the church's story. These things are nearly indisputable. What is a matter of concern is the translation of that impulse by faulty and flawed human organizations and institutions. The colonial legacy of White superiority, European certainty, cultural forms being merged with spiritual ones, and the marriage of economic influences with theological enterprises requires a critical analysis. Otherwise, the danger of replicating and re-creating these harmful and hierarchical power dynamics will result in reinforcing the very structures and attitudes that the gospel calls us to expose and work to dismantle.

Neomonastic communities and practices have made quite a return during the past decades. Consumer culture is unceasing and unsatisfying. Technology can be wonderful but it can also be isolating and exhausting. Urban life can wear on a soul and create a unique kind of loneliness in the midst of so much activity and chaos. These are just a few of the reasons that some have chosen to attempt to reclaim ancient practices and intentional community. For some it provides a retreat and for others it comes as a protest to these same factors. Christ wants more from us and for us than to consume, punch the clock, sit in traffic, and stare at screens.

Historic practices of the church's past hold a great deal of attraction to those who want a way out or who want to abstain via a form of protest that can result in the formation of personal character and community in ways that stand in stark contrast to a life of busyness, fractured attention, competing loyalties, and broken relationships. Different communities utilize schedules of prayer, practices of Sabbath rest, personal reflection, intentional reading of Scripture (such as *lectio divina*), communal meals, and commitments to simplicity as a deliberate expression of countercultural values.

The danger of any past-looking project is not simply in attempting to replicate a romanticized notion of a previous era (as desirable as that may be). The greater danger is participating in unexamined forms and mentalities that were embedded within larger historical structures. Practices do not emerge out of a vacuum but instead are born out of context and a situation. They are inherently situated, and while they may be appropriated for a different time and location, they are not neutral and do not come without embedded values.

While the appeal of opting out of, retreating or abstaining from the modern consumer culture may be understandable, one must be careful to avoid operating out of one's inherited privilege or as a consumer of religious experience.[16] Awareness of and participation in practices of past centuries are understandably attractive in our world of alienation, discouragement, and resignation. One must be careful, however, not to use those practices to escape from or to avoid the histories of oppression, marginalization, and injustice found in previous centuries, or else one will reinforce the imperial structures that one is attempting to avoid or protest.

These three contemporary trends in Christianity are emblematic of directions within many programs, movements, groups, and organizations. The danger is that any reclamation, renovation, or reformation project that does

16. That one has the ability to exercise the option of opting out or of protesting may be due to one's relative privilege. If living this way is one of many options that an individual may choose between, there is an inherent danger of replicating the very consumer choice that one is attempting to avoid or protest. This same concern could be applied to the trend of disenchanted Evangelicals becoming Catholic, Anglican, or Orthodox. Unless the capitalist context has been accounted for, the consumer nature of making choices will continue to infect and corrupt even this quest for theological or ecclesiastic purity.

not account for postcolonial concerns may replicate and reinforce the very things that the gospel calls us to combat. It would be tragic if, due to a lack of attention and intention regarding colonial mentalities, the honest impulse and honorable motive of these innovative and energizing approaches were to unintentionally re-create the hurtful and harmful effects they are seeking to escape. The tools and resources available to anticolonial and decolonial work are vital for the task at hand and will be increasingly valuable in our lifetime as racial tensions, global markets, and environmental degradation continue to be issues.

3

Historic Postcolonial Theologies

Randy: Okay. This has been really informative, but some of us, perhaps, lack the background to appreciate postcolonial theology, especially the language used in discussing postcolonial theory. Take me, for example. Even though I have been decolonizing my own mind and critiquing Evangelical theology for many years, I am not as versed in the language of postcolonial theory as you. Can you take some time to introduce me and others to some of the basic constructs?

Bo: I am happy to try to do that! One of the most intimidating (and exhilarating) aspects of entering into postcolonial conversation is encountering new words, concepts, and thinkers. Concepts such as *Americanity, mimicry, tricontinental, subaltern,* and *Orientalism* provide new ways to address big concepts while ensuring that it is not the inherited traditional/colonial perspective that is unintentionally reinforced.

One may ask, Is all the new vocabulary necessary? If you want to challenge the way that people think or want to approach a situation from a different angle, there are several options as to how to utilize words and concepts: modify and invent new words or challenge the dominant use of a word. Going the *new words* route is more difficult initially because it can create a barrier to the uninitiated person's ability to participate. A steep learning curve can be intimidating but there is an upside. Going the *redefinition* route provides an entry point that is initially more accessible but might ultimately prove more draining, as the common use provides inherent resistance.

In the end, if one only uses the words and concepts of the established order, it may be difficult to provide the level of impact and critique required. The given nature of the assumed order may require vocabulary and conceptual frameworks developed outside of the current system if one wants to escape the dominant view. Of course, the danger is the creation of an elitist system of those "in the know," which can feel exclusionary of those communities most heavily impacted by the colonial structure. Regardless of this danger, the reality of the dilemma is that most postcolonial trailblazers have decided to employ new words in order to use the weapons of the colonial system of knowledge and control against itself. Many have pressed into the ultra-academic legitimacy in order to wrest control of the discourse away from its traditional gatekeepers. For this reason alone, I think we are obligated to expose people to these "new words."

So, for the purpose of this book, I am going to embrace this postcolonial tendency so people can follow the lead of those who have established and defined the field. In order to conceive of the world as being and working in a different way, I will adopt and adapt some new concepts and vocabulary. These new words provide a way of interrogating the given order, and they challenge the assumed structures of power and control. Still, I venture up this trail with great concern. I want to avoid re-creating a new kind of elitism and reinforcing the very hierarchical structure that rewards those at the top to the detriment and exclusion of those on the underside.

The nature of postcolonial work means that unlike other fields, there is no "canon" per se, and one has to be careful when holding up key figures in a "hall of fame" sort of way. Any such list will be examined with a critical lens and scrutinized with the concerns covered in the previous chapter. Locating oneself and naming one's program are vital for this reason. There is no "generic" or "regular," and so meaning is seen to be both contested and constructed. Entering into postcolonial conversation and thought intrinsically necessitates a reflexive posture as to one's voice and perspective, assumptions, operative narratives, social location, and agenda or program.

Randy: Okay, how about you start by naming some of the major figures in the history and development of postcolonial thought?[1]

Bo: I'll attempt to provide a quick orientation to the field with this survey and to initiate people into some of the broader concerns. This list is not total, nor are the summaries comprehensive. That's because this book is meant to be an introduction for students, and as such our overview should be basic, focusing specifically on aspects that will prepare the reader for a more constructive proposal. (To the reader: One helpful exercise may be for you to highlight or keep a list of all new terms and names unfamiliar

---

1. At this point, we hope you are beginning to question our suggestions as well: "Who did they name? Who did they leave out? What is the narrative they are constructing?" If this is the case, we are glad you are catching on!

to you. If we mention them, we think they are important for you to know.)

Edward Said (pronounced: sy-EED) is credited with initiating the current postcolonial approach with his work on Orientalism. Said, who was Palestinian, used classic literature to show the ways in which British colonizers had created, or invented, an "other" out of the Middle East and India. It is impossible to overstate how influential Said has been; even those who are most critical of his work are paying great attention to it.[2] Said demonstrates how Europeans created a construct of difference in order to define themselves over and against the East.

The Arab world, the Orient, and the West are all constructed or imagined creations that functioned to give colonizers a static canvas on which to portray themselves and their cultures as superior and advanced. The Orient was dark, exotic, and mysterious (among other things), but most of all it was *essential* and static. The colonized were not agents with their own subjectivities but objects to be studied, controlled, and represented by the Western voice and perspective. In contrast to the occidental West, it was said that oriental peoples were primitive, backward, and set.

Said's work opened a door that exposed two explosively controversial implications for the *civilized* world. The first impact was to strip the veil of innocence that had been presumed by traditional fields ranging from anthropology and mapmaking to literature and missiology. The second impact established that the colonial exercise of power and

2. Critics of Said say that his work did not go far enough or deep enough due to the literary focus, or that it was primarily focused on Western literature without acknowledging resistance literature. Latin American critics point out that Spanish colonization of the seventeenth century was very different from British colonization in the nineteenth and that Latin American emancipation was achieved more than a century before World War II.

control was not just in land and military domination but extended also to the production of knowledge. Domination and control extended to an assault on indigenous ways of knowing (what academics call epistemological violence), narratives (such as origin stories), as well as language.

Gayatri Chakravorty Spivak, a scholar from India, raised one of the most important questions in the development of the field: Can the subaltern speak?[3] In her writing is found a profound critique of colonial mentalities. Spivak masters the tools of the colonizers in thought and vocabulary in order to use those very constructs against them. Some have been critical of her work because it is too erudite and because her writing style is so elaborate and intricate.

Spivak uses *subaltern* from the work of critical theorist Antonio Gramsci to signify the marginalized groups who are presumed and whose subjectivity is denied by Western scholarship. The theme of epistemology (ways of knowing) is important because European philosophy (such as the metaphysics of Hegel and Kant) was imposed by colonial authors in a way that silenced the non-colonial voice. This epistemic violence (as Foucalt called it) renders the colonized as an object of study that is represented by the imposed categories of the colonizer. When communities are stripped of their subjectivity, their ways of knowing, histories, experiences, insights, and perspectives are silenced and made into objects of study. No longer afforded a subjectivity of their own, they are analyzed and subsequently represented in terms of the imposed colonial categorizations. Like Said, Spivak also utilized literary analysis to expose the production of the other.

3 Spivak published an influential essay by this title. Spivak, "Can the Subaltern Speak?," in Nelson and Grossberg, *Marxism and the Interpretation of Culture*, 271–313.

Aimé Césaire wrote *Discours sur le colonialisme* (*Discourse on Colonialism*), which, though composed in a unique poetic style, contained a vicious critique and was read as a manifesto. From French Martinique, Césaire contended that colonialism cannot be seen as a benevolent enterprise conducted out of selflessness and kindness. Colonialism was not done to improve the lives of the colonized; it was done out of selfishness and economic motivation. Colonies were established and exploited with a veneer of Christian goodness, but in the end they created distinct racial and economic problems. Césaire argued that any civilization that was corrupt enough to have a hand in colonialism was already rotten, and this can be seen in the barbarism with which colonized natives were treated:

> First we must study how colonization works to *decivilize* the colonizer, to *brutalize* him in the true sense of the word, to degrade him, to awaken him to buried instincts, to covetousness, violence, race hatred, and moral relativism. . . . A universal regression takes place, a gangrene sets in, a center of infection begins to spread; and . . . at the end of all these treaties that have been violated, all these lies that have been propagated, all these punitive expeditions that have been tolerated, all these prisoners who have been tied up and "interrogated," all these patriots who have been tortured, at the end of all the racial pride that has been encouraged, all the boastfulness that has been displayed, a poison has been distilled into the veins of Europe and, slowly but surely, the continent proceeds toward *savagery*.[4]

Césaire is important for our project here because, as introduced in the previous chapter, many of us in the dominant

4. Césaire, *Discourse on Colonialism*, 35–36.

culture need to be disabused of the sanitized narratives we have inherited. The narrative sterilizes the undesirable elements of our history as unfortunate but probably necessary aspects of the way that things came to be. Defenders of the status quo say that while certain activities or mentalities may not be desirable now, that was just the way things were back then, and look at the good that came out of it! Negative dialectics do not let history off the hook that easily. We don't need to whitewash history and accept that horrible but often used phrase "This is just the way things are."

The work of Césaire exhorts us not to turn a blind eye to the motives of colonial missions or to accept the party line that ultimately more good came out of colonialism than bad—and that it was done out of a pure heart, even if there were some ugly elements and regrettable episodes. The critical lens says the dark parts are as telling as the highlights, the unreasonable elements cannot be hidden behind the label "age of reason," and the savagery and barbarism of genocide and slavery call into question the civilizing efforts of the era.

> Because it is a systematic negation of the other person and a furious determination to deny the other person all the attributes of humanity, colonialism forces the people it dominates to ask themselves the question constantly: "in reality, who am I?"

—Frantz Fanon[5]

Frantz Fanon's *Wretched of the Earth* serves as a battle cry from the underside of history. Born in Martinique, he argues that the colonial world is divided and compartmentalized; in order for change to happen within the whole social order, it must be changed from the bottom up.

5. Fanon, *Wretched of the Earth*, 250.

Decolonization, to Fanon, is always a violent enterprise and is always a program of complete disorder. The purported order, peace, and security so prized in modern society are a facade erected to hide the ugly underside of violence, which was employed to establish the supposed peaceful order.

Fanon's comfort with violence may be objectionable to some followers of Jesus; however, the point that cannot be missed is that the colonizer's imposition of external categories and the resultant compartmentalization are a form of control and oppression. In order to address this dominating mechanism, destruction of those heavily policed categories is essential. This is a chaotic process that challenges the established "order" and will inherently result in a form of disorder. Fannon's assertions may be more acceptable to the novice once Spivak's insight about marginalized subjects and Césaire's challenge of benevolent motive have been integrated.

In *Black Skin, White Masks*, Fanon exposes the Manichaean nature of the colonial world. Manichaeism, in this sense, is a moral dualism in which everything is divided between its two natures: light and dark, good and evil, civilized and savage, love and hate, fact and myth. Fanon had begun to address this theme in *Wretched of the Earth*:

> This world divided into compartments, this world cut in two is inhabited by two different species. The originality of the colonial context is that economic reality, inequality, and the immense difference of ways of life never come to mask the human realities. When you examine at close quarters the colonial context, it is evident that what parcels out the world is to begin with the fact of belonging to or not belonging to a given race, a given species.[6]

6. Fanon, *Wretched of the Earth*, 39–40.

Homi Bhabha, who was born in Mumbai, India, is credited with two dynamic concepts that have recently come into popular use: *mimicry* and *hybridity*. Mimicry can be thought of as a process of imitation, repetition, and authentication that results in a "like-but-not-quite" expression. Bhabha exposes the inherent problem with the "not quite/ not white" limitation of mimicry. The nature of mimicry is that it is never quite the same and thus has a built-in drift or slippage to it that is perpetually creating variations and deviation. Each new level of mimicry is attempting to gain elusive validation and, in so doing, generating novel expressions that are never quite the same as the desired.

The discursive nature of the colonial project results in a "not quite the same" status that subsequently must be mediated and navigated. This process is called *hybridity*, and it addresses the way that cultural identities are impacted and transformed via contact between the colonized and the colonizer. The contact zone between groups and communities is a contested space and is in constant flux. Identities of both groups must adjust, adapt, and evolve due to the mutually transforming nature of the interaction. Knowledge and power are not established in a vacuum, nor do they remain static.

In Said, Spivak, Césaire, Fanon, and Bhabha we have five figures that any student would encounter in an introductory course on postcolonialism. Their work does not form the beginning of a canon per se, but they do provide a sound entry point to the field of postcolonial studies.

Randy: Exactly the kind of background I was hoping you would provide! Can we cross over to postcolonial theologians now?

Bo: Definitely! More recently, both biblical scholarship and theology have come into more pronounced conversation with postcolonial approaches. Bringing postcolonial theory into theological and biblical studies is exhilarating at one level—opening up the field to an interdisciplinary arena—and difficult due to the embedded presumptions within so much of the inherited tradition. Hesitancy and even resistance by established disciplines is to be anticipated due to the nature of postcolonialism's concerns and intrinsic critique. R. S. Sugirtharajah and Musa Dube (pronounced doo-bay) are two representative figures that demonstrate the powerful dynamic of postcolonial approaches to their respective fields.

Musa Dube authored *Postcolonial Feminist Interpretation of the Bible*, and it stands alongside many recent works from feminist and womanist scholars who have opened the eyes of many to the possibilities of diverse perspectives for reading the Bible. Her work has also exposed the problems and limitations of colonial readings of the Bible. Originally from Botswana, she introduces her book with a well-known African dictum:

> When the white man came to our country he had the Bible and we had the land. The white man said to us, "let us pray." After the prayer, the white man had the land and we had the Bible.[7]

Dube goes on to demonstrate how traditional ways of reading the Bible are both hierarchical and hurtful to groups in other parts of the world. These oppressive consequences are not only exposed and addressed but an alternative is provided that attends to the needs of communities in the two-thirds world and of the women in them, specifically. She demonstrates how a reading of the gospel of Matthew can have a decolonizing effect and work to undo the imperial structures that it has historically been used to support.

7. Dube, *Postcolonial Feminist Interpretation*, 3.

R. S. Sugirtharajah has contributed works like *Voices from the Margin* and *Asian Faces of Jesus*, but it is *Postcolonial Criticism and Biblical Interpretation* that demonstrates how, as he explains, the field "opens up potential areas for biblical studies to work in tandem with other disciplines."[8] Though he is originally from Sri Lanka, he incorporates and points to work happening in Latin America, Asia, and Africa, among other places. He celebrates the arrival of postcolonial criticism because it counters the prevailing European rationalism and pietism and enables biblical scholars to bring their own questions to the text instead of wrestling with the inherited questions that held no interest.

According to Sugirtharajah, postcolonial biblical criticism provides an emancipatory permission to leave behind the tyranny of Western biblical scholarship and to approach Scripture with the same kinds of questions as any other critical practice:

- What is a text?
- Who produced it?
- How is its meaning determined?
- How is it circulated?
- Who interprets it?
- Who are the beneficiaries of the interpretation?
- What were the circumstances of the production?
- Does a text have any message?
- If so, what sort?[9]

8. Sugirtharajah, *Postcolonial Criticism and Biblical Interpretation*, 25.

9. Sugirtharajah, *Exploring Postcolonial Biblical Criticism*, 2.

Questions like these begin to take on a question-behind-the-question quality. One significant difference, potentially, is that critical theory often employs a "hermeneutic of suspicion." This is often done in an attempt at deconstruction. Sugirtharajah models the potential of doing this work while employing a "hermeneutic of generosity" in an attempt at a constructive approach. These two approaches, obviously, are not mutually exclusive, and some dismantling may need to happen in order to create space for the constructive project.

Among the many difficult topics that Sugirtharajah tackles fearlessly is the painful and complicated question of whether the Bible is an anti-imperial or an empire-endorsing text. He diligently exposes the ways in which the Bible has passages of both types and also has a subsequent history of interpretations that support both.

Separating the Layers of Colonialism

Postcolonial scholars often employ elaborate frameworks in order to challenge and dismantle embedded assumptions related to racism (White supremacy) and colonizing structures. It is important to note that constructs are not monolithic—they do not necessarily originate or draw power from the same sources—and neither do they impact communities or concerns uniformly. Three interrelated but distinct manifestations in colonialism are

1. slaveability/anti-Black racism, which anchors capitalism;

2. genocide, which anchors colonialism; and

3. orientalism, which anchors war.[10]

10. Smith, "Indigeneity, Settler Colonialism, White Supremacy."

These three constructions are utilized in distinct ways and affect communities diversely. Taken together they reinforce each other for a mutated or exponential impact but must be understood as both distinct in their origin and diverse/multiple in their effect and impact.[11] The Western European conception of race and our current form of capitalism grew up together within colonialism's frameworks. Understanding the ways in which these *couplings* inform and empower one another is essential for each aspect of the three layers of the colonial legacy.[12]

Analyzing the above three pillars of colonialism is expanded and compounded even more with the addition of different eras and subsequent evolutions of colonialism. This added layer of *time* is not intended to make things more complicated or more difficult to address any one aspect—quite the opposite! Understanding the multilayered and ongoing adaptations of the colonial legacy is essential to peeling back the assumed nature of things and exposing the underlying factors. Exposing and examining the historical, philosophical, economic, religious, racial, territorial, and legal roots provides a powerful avenue for calling into question the inherited structures that continue to evolve and adapt in order to stay operative in our era.

Americanity is a concept developed by sociologists Aníbal Quijano and Immanuel Wallerstein, who write that "for the first three centuries of the modern world-system, all the states in the Americas were formal colonies,

---

11. The danger of adopting a one-size-fits-all approach that portrays racism (White supremacy) as singular in origin and uniform in expression or impact is that it does not account for the trifold nature of the system's configuration.

12. Martin Luther King Jr.'s triplets of evil—racism, poverty, and militarism—provide a proto-view of this same phenomenon.

subordinated politically to a few European ones."[13] This was to change in a significant way. Those colonies under Iberian rule (Spanish and Portuguese) and those under British rule were to go through a transformative adaptation in which they became two different monsters that must be confronted differently. These authors point out that the formal end of colonialism brought a certain level of independence but it did not undo coloniality; it merely transformed its outer form. The recent transformation into nongovernmental organizations, transnational corporations, paramilitary operations, and missions agencies (to name only a few forms) is as important to understanding postcolonial theory as lingering mentalities from the fifteenth or sixteenth century are.

Americanity

Randy: I think this is an important concept for us all to grasp when speaking in our particular context of historic colonialism. Can you say more about it?

Bo: Current social structures of ethnicity and ethnic hierarchy are overriding remnants from the colonial legacy. At the end of formal slavery in the nineteenth century, America became "the first state in the modern system to enact formal segregation. This development was in addition to being the first country to put Native Americans in reserves."[14] These two moves are notable both in their innovation and in their enduring impact. When one considers the barbarism and savagery of the age of exploration typified in the conquistadores, it is shocking to think of the systematized brutality that came with these developments

13. Quijano and Wallerstein, "Americanity as a Concept," 550.
14. Quijano and Wallerstein, "Americanity as a Concept," 551.

in which "formal racism became a further contribution of Americanity to the world-system."[15]

According to Quijano and Wallerstein, the British followed the Iberian exploration by about a century, and the developments of the sixteenth century (banking practices, world market, capitalism, modernity) are the first keys to understanding the important distinction between the two zones of North America in contrast to Latin and South America. "The arrival of the British to the northern parts of America more than a century later took place when this new historical process was already fully underway. Consequently, the colonizing societies were radically different from each other, as would be the modalities of colonization and its implications for the respective metropoles and colonial societies."[16]

It was in the seventeenth century that the European situation shifted radically (royal dynasties, eastern trade, competition with the French, Dutch, and others); both Spain and Portugal were marginalized in a significant way. These commercial considerations impacted a societal shift in the colonies that rested on conceptions imported with the conquistadores. To inflame matters, political realities back in Spain (such as the introduction of the Bourbon dynasty) demanded greater material production from the colonies while weakening both the trade allegiance of the colonies and setting up the eventual political structure that would manifest in an un-unified identity and expression.

In British-America there was no state church that was all-powerful as there had been in Spain during the Inquisition. The Inquisition had served to hold off modernity and what came to be called rationality in Ibero-America before

15. Quijano and Wallerstein, "Americanity as a Concept," 551.
16. Quijano and Wallerstein, "Americanity as a Concept," 553.

the Bourbons.[17] Further contrasts between the structures, mentalities, and technologies of industrialization highlight how significant a difference that century made between the Iberian (Spanish-Portuguese) and the British approaches. The fracturing political realities meant that by the nineteenth century there was no central power capable of organizing a unified identity or coalition as in the former Ibero-zone. The contrast to the centralized and increasingly industrialized North Atlantic trade and identity conception (British-North America) is stark—they are imagined as permanent foreign threats to empire.

The important distinction in history and in mentality between the two zones (Iberian and British) sheds light on why ongoing atrocities have been visited on the indigenes—who have not been widely assimilated, nor have they been legitimized. This change is attributed to the difference between the Iberian mentality of colonies as societies where Europeans mixed with natives versus the British mindset of "European-societies-outside-of-Europe." Quijano and Wallerstein point out that the British were unique to call these societies "nations" and after America's independence (from its original colonial power) to "exterminate rather than to colonize the Native Americans."[18] The devastating distinction comes to light: as rival nations they are not to be assimilated or absorbed but perpetually relinquished and destroyed. This distinction holds deep ramification for postcolonial exchanges between minority communities in North America and the work coming from Latin and South America.

The ongoing imperial expansion of the American military, economy, and ideology places minority communities within its first-world boundaries. In post–Cold War

17. Quijano and Wallerstein, "Americanity as a Concept," 555.
18. Quijano and Wallerstein, "Americanity as a Concept," 552.

vernacular, these concerns were often relegated as third-world perspectives. Recently, they have been identified as the two-thirds world. The possibility of being akin to fourth-world status (third world within first world) is plausible in this scenario. When scholars and activists engage from this location, then, their contribution is difficult to classify, especially in comparison to those originating in Latin and South America or elsewhere in the two-thirds world.

Layering postcolonial analysis in this way is vital. Addressing racial, economic, religious, territorial, and militaristic issues is more than any one project can do at one time. The situation is too complex and too elaborate to examine all at once. With the addition of different and evolving eras of colonialism and colonial approaches, it becomes nearly impossible to survey the entire spectrum in any coherent way. Decolonial and anticolonial work employs strategies, including some of the tools that we have explored in this and the previous chapter, in order to focus the critique for maximum impact. The colonial legacy is deeply rooted, often assumed as a default, and thus its impact continues to be pervasive in our era. Postcolonial conversation bridges academic approaches and grassroots communities, voices from the center and the margin, history and theory, activism and advocacy, politics and religion.

Okay, this turned out to be much more of a one-way conversation than I imagined (and for the reader's insight, much more edited). How about I ask some more questions of you?

Randy: Okay, but first I want you to address two other important historical lenses concerning Evangelicalism and give just a bit of critique, if you will.

Bo: Alright, what are they?

Randy: Can you talk about the two major Quadrilaterals often discussed in Evangelicalism, those of Bebbington and Wesley?

Bo: Sure, but you know this stuff too. How about you discuss Bebbington's Quadrilateral and then I'll talk about Wesley's Quadrilateral?

Randy: I suppose that's fair.

Randy: In most Evangelical circles, the name of contemporary British scholar David Bebbington is known because of his overall definition of what makes an Evangelical. As the term *Quadrilateral* suggests, there are four major areas he posits, and I suspect 98 percent of all Evangelicals subscribe to these in one way or another and to various degrees. This first is *biblicism*, which asserts that all essential spiritual truth is to be found in the Bible. The second is *crucicentrism*, which directs attention to the atoning work of Jesus on the cross. The third is *conversionism*, the belief that people need to be converted to Christ. The fourth and last, *activism*, is the belief that the gospel needs to be spread to others. My critique of these is straightforward—first of all, the Bible.

Biblicism: The Bible is not one book but many books that contain many stories—in fact, it's about 90 percent stories, written by premodern peoples. The West's inability to access an understanding of story familiar to many Indigenous peoples sets it at a disadvantage. The Western approach is to search for discoverable facts in the Bible and assert propositions. I don't think most of the books in the Bible were ever intended to be read this way. Indigenous people, on the other hand, are used to hearing story. The story will contain truth of some kind, even if it is a story showing us how not to act. For Indigenous peoples, the meaning of the stories can even change given the circumstances and context in which they find themselves. Even though the Western mind tries to approach the Bible as one book, containing all truth for all time, what Westerners really are doing is selecting the portions that match their theology and disregarding other portions that do not. In this sense, the West can claim a unifying and universal truth that supersedes any local theologies.

Crucicentrism: My problem with crucicentrism is that it focuses on the death of Jesus on the cross to the neglect of the other aspects of his life like his incarnation, the deliberate kind of life he lived, his message, his resurrection, his current status, and his role as Creator. When one aspect of the whole Jesus story is lifted above the others, it does not do justice to the sacrifices and choices and whole purpose of the story. In fact, Evangelicals have lifted up his death and belief in the atonement to the point where subscribing to a certain belief about it determines, they believe, who will spend eternity in heaven and who will spend eternity in hell. I'm quite certain that Jesus did not live and die simply to be the eternal judge of the righteous and the damned.

Conversionism: While I do believe people should become converted to walk and talk with Jesus, I'm pretty sure that there is not a particular way that happens. A Native American elder once told me a story of his uncle, who lived to be 108 years old and had never been to church or been taught Bible stories, and yet was always informing him about Jesus and his ways. His uncle told him, "Never disrespect Jesus—he is a Great Spirit, and I talk to him." The elder told me one day he decided to ask his uncle why he knew so much about Jesus. His uncle replied, "I told you, I talk to him." The elder replied, "But how do you know what he says and does?" The elder told me his uncle looked at him quizzically, and then replied, "Don't you think he talks back to me?" Life, and relationship with anyone, especially Creator, is full of many conversions, and at many levels. Thank God we don't all have to do it in the same way!

Activism: I think most Evangelicals understand this as evangelism, which usually means sharing one's faith. I believe we should all share our spiritual experiences when asked, if we think our experience might help someone else draw closer to Great Mystery and live a better life on earth. A wise elder and friend of seventy-two years of age once told me, "I don't recall ever giving my opinion about anything, to anyone, when it was not asked for, where anything positive ever came of it." I'll leave it at that.

Randy: Now, how about Wesley's Quadrilateral? (Funny how these things come in fours, eh?)

Bo: Lots of good things come in fours: four winds, four seasons, four directions, even four gospels! It seems to help humans think of balance and stability while acknowledging change.

This quadrilateral of values provides an amazing framework for personal faith and communal discernment. It is probably the most helpful tool that I have found for spiritual/religious thinking and discussion in the twenty-first century.

There are three important issues to understand about this Wesleyan quadrilateral that illuminate the core elements themselves. The first issue is related to Scripture. Wesley, being from the Anglican tradition, held to *prima scriptura*—Scripture first. This position was in contrast to the more famous (and dominant) position held by many Reformation-era Protestants of *sola scriptura*—Scripture alone. This distinction provides a significant contrast from more fundamentalist approaches that descended from the Reformation.

The second issue relates to experience. Methodists, by adding "experience" to their quadrilateral, depart from the inherited Anglican tripartite formulation of Scripture, tradition, and reason. This recognition of the importance of experience is a key distinction that transforms the formulation from a merely cerebral approach to inherited religious frameworks to a vibrant expectation of personal application and a clear recognition that a community's (or person's) experience of the divine is a valid location for God's revelation and our reflection. We recognize the importance of people's concrete lived realities and not just a set of ideas or abstract speculations and theories. This is especially true when considering the underrepresented voices that have traditionally been marginalized or repressed in Christian history.

The third issue deals with sequence. The four elements of the "quad" are not perfectly parallel. In fact, I think that this formation works best when addressed in this sequence. We start with scripture because it provides us a starting point and trajectory for the revelation of God's work in the world. We don't start with experience because faith does not begin with us. There is a *givenness* to the faith that we have inherited. That is why we look to the tradition next. We don't lead with reason either because ours is a faith tradition centered on incarnation—the embodied presence of the divine—and not merely ideas, concepts, and theories.

My favorite way to present the quadrilateral is to temporarily remove each one and examine how the construct would be impoverished without its presence.

Scripture: Try to imagine a religion or faith that had tradition, experience, and reason. It might still hold together and provide communities and people with direction and connection. It would, however, be lacking something vital and central to the entire enterprise.

93

Scripture provides us with an essential framework for our belief and practice. This is done through the use of narrative and example. The framing stories given to us in Scripture are vitally important both for the precedent that they provide us and for the trajectory they set in expectation for faithful (and faith-filled) continuation.

Tradition: Without tradition we would be left to try to read this antiquated text that has been translated into modern language and to attempt to import and apply it in our contemporary context without any framework or guidance. Tradition provides us an example of practices, behaviors, approaches, relationships, and applications that we can learn from and be enriched by. This is available to us in both the positive of what to do and the negative of what to avoid. Without tradition we are left with only trial and error and we are poorer without the exemplars of the faith.

Experience: A faith that is not experienced is an empty shell—a corpse with no life in it. The church was birthed in Pentecost and it is Holy Spirit power that animates her life still. This faith must be experienced and allowed to transform our incarnated (embodied and enacted) expressions of it.

Reason: We live at the far end of Christian history and know well the dangers of an unreasonable faith. Heresies, cults, and genocidal atrocities are the result. We learn a great deal from the legacy of these tragic consequences.

I appreciate the Wesleyan quad so much. It is a wonderful rubric for running ideas through and a helpful diagnostic for communal (or corporate) discussions and decision-making. I do, however, see that it has two limitations. The first is that it is constructed. It is a construct that was developed in the late 1970s by well-meaning Methodists who were in need of such a tool.[19] That doesn't

19. Albert C. Outler is generally credited with initiating use of the

mean that it is wrong, or flawed, only that it, like so many other things, is a man-made device. It is found nowhere in Wesley's writings or earlier Methodist material. So, as we have been practicing, we have to ask the question behind the question: Why did this idea need to be created three hundred years after Wesley's writing? What was the need and how does this construct address that need? What is its purpose or function?

The second and more consequential concern is that there is an unspoken modifier that is often presumed before each of the four elements: Christian Scripture, Christian tradition, European/Western reason, and Christian experience. The Wesleyan quadrilateral would be challenged by notions of Hindu scriptures, Indigenous traditions, alternative "ways of knowing," and experiences via Native ceremonies.

So while there can be great value in the Wesleyan quad, we need to make sure that it is not employed in order to reinforce colonial Christianity. It would be tragic if this constructive and liberative tool was used to colonize *others'* experiences of the divine-transcendent.

---

quadrilateral formulation.

4

Developing a Postcolonial Worldview Where You Stand

Creator of the Land

Bo: Since you've mentioned spirituality, in your own way of thinking, how do you draw parallels between following Jesus and maintaining your sense of Native American spirituality?

Randy: Christians, at least first-century Christians, believed Christ was already present in other cultures via his work as Creator. Therefore, it's paramount that as we are thinking in postcolonial theological terms, when discussing Jesus' shalom mission, especially when reflecting on his divinity, we acknowledge that according to several writers in the New Testament, Jesus the man is also recognized as Christ, the divine Creator. After spending time with Jesus, or knowing those who did, I don't think the writers of the New Testament felt they had any other choice except to proclaim his unique status as divine.

Bo: Okay, so, in your mind, what are the theological implications of that understanding?

Randy: Well, first of all I think we need to ask ourselves why Christians, especially Evangelicals, have been so reluctant to make the same proclamation.

Bo: Whoa! So, you think there is a disconnect here?

Randy: Exactly! I think the classic Western theology concerning salvation is so tightly wound that Christians have had to create a binary in their thinking in this regard. Jesus can't be Creator because he is the savior. The Father or Parent-God can't be crucified because he is the Creator. And the Spirit, well . . . Spirit is so amorphous in most theologies that we just tack Spirit on anywhere we chose.

Bo: Okay, so this sounds really important. Could you break all this down in detail?

Randy: Okay. Notice that the literary structure of New Testament references to Christ as Creator are predominantly in formulaic style, meaning they may have been mnemonic devices, memorized as poems or sung as hymns. These formulaic patterns suggest that the early Jewish understanding of Christ as Creator somehow equated Jesus with YHWH and that it was a popular theme in the early church. Here is the account found in the Gospel of John:

> In the beginning the Word already existed.
> The Word was with God,
> and the Word was God.
> He existed in the beginning with God.
> God created everything through him,
> and nothing was created except through him.

97

> The Word gave life to everything that was created,
>
> and his life brought light to everyone.
> (John 1:1–4 NLT)

In the writer's mind, Jesus is preexistent—in some way having divine origins. The writer understood Jesus as God's instrument in creation and as giving life to all creation. In the same chapter, verses 10–14, the writer speaks of God's redemptive value in Christ. The writer seems to have a fluid understanding of Jesus the man and Jesus the preexistent Christ, who is somehow also Creator. The writer of the Gospel of John also appears to understand the very same Jesus as the redeemer of all things. In a formulaic pattern similar to the one found in John's Gospel, the Apostle Paul writes,

> Christ is the visible image of the invisible God.
>
> He existed before anything was created and is supreme over all creation,
>
> for through him God created everything in the heavenly realms and on earth.
>
> He made the things we can see and the things we can't see—such as thrones, kingdoms, rulers, and authorities in the unseen world.
>
> Everything was created through him and for him.
>
> He existed before anything else,
>
> and he holds all creation together.
>
> Christ is also the head of the church,
>
> which is his body.
>
> He is the beginning,
>
> supreme over all who rise from the dead.
>
> So he is first in everything.

> For God in all his fullness
>
> was pleased to live in Christ,
>
> and through him God reconciled
>
> everything to himself.
>
> He made peace with everything in heaven
> and on earth
>
> by means of Christ's blood on the cross.
> (Col 1:15–20 NLT)

In this text Paul understands

- Christ as preexistent;
- Christ as having supremacy over all creation;
- Christ as God's instrument in creation;
- all creation as being created by Christ;
- all creation as made for Christ; and
- Christ making shalom with all creation by his redemptive death.

Paul's explanation parallels John's understanding of Christ the Human, Christ the Creator, and Christ the Redeemer. Paul references another formulaic description of Christ as Creator in 1 Corinthians 8:6:

> But we know that there is only one God, the Father, who created everything, and we live for him. And there is only one Lord, Jesus Christ, through whom God made everything and through whom we have been given life. (NLT)

Once again, Paul states that through Jesus, God made all creation, and through him we all have life.

A fourth reference, possibly constructed in a similar kind of formula, is found in the Letter to the Hebrews:

> Long ago God spoke many times and in many
> ways to our ancestors through the prophets.
> And now in these final days, he has spoken to
> us through his Son. God promised everything to
> the Son as an inheritance, and through the Son
> he created the universe. (Heb 1:1–2 NLT)

As with the other passages, the writer of Hebrews begins by reasoning that, through Christ, God created all of creation and that all creation belongs to him. Later, the same writer ties the creation act to Christ's redemptive actions by saying, "For it was fitting that he, for whom and by whom all things exist, in bringing many sons to glory, should make the founder of their salvation perfect through suffering" (Heb 2:10 ESV).

In this great mystery of incarnation and reconciliation, those who walked with or near the incarnate Christ came to an understanding that he was the orchestrator of creation. Without a better understanding of God's plan through Jesus Christ as both Creator and Savior/Reconciler (shalom bringer), the modern church has overzealously developed a severely imbalanced salvation/healing theology that favors otherworldliness over physical realities. Even the Trinity, which in Christian theology has traditionally been seen as an ethereal subject, is rooted and grounded both in creation and in the crucifixion.[1]

---

1. The idea of physical *place* should not be overlooked even when referencing the Trinity. Also, the fingerprint (or DNA) of God is on all creation, allowing Trinitarian concepts to become tangible and accessible. For a detailed philosophical article on panentheism, please see the article by that title in the Stanford Encyclopedia of Philosophy, available at http://plato.stanford.edu/entries/panentheism/. For a more complete historical theology, see McDonough, *Christ as Creator: Origins of a New Testament Doctrine.*

Bo: Why is it important that this form of postcolonial theology urge Evangelicals to recognize Christ as Creator?

Randy: As a settler-colonial society the West has placed an emphasis on *time* to the deprecation of serious thinking concerning *place*. The emphasis on time over place naturally bends Christianity toward an abstract trajectory, to the point where theology and practical theology (including missiology) become two distinct realities. This classic dualism is at the heart of many Western theologies, reflecting an empire-driven foundation.

Just Land

Bo: We both think place is so important when it comes to grounding faith. Can you speak more specifically about place as the basis of postcolonial theologies?

Randy: The Creator of all things is also the reconciler of all things, and all things (read: all creation) are being created for Christ. Paul, in the Colossians passage, even says Christ "holds all things together." Since all things are redeemed in Christ, then restoring the world to God's intentions of shalom is the point of Christ's redemption. In a very real sense, Christ restores harmony back to our lives, our world, and our universe. The basic issue at stake in our day is perhaps the breadth of healing God has made available in Christ. If Jesus died for all creation, and not just the human "soul," and not even just for humans (but for "all things"), then the concept of redemption is much broader than many Western theologians have traditionally thought.

Redemption (our salvation/healing) is reconciliation of and for the whole earth.[2]

Bo: And concerning Native Americans?

Randy: Maybe Martin King said it best:

> Our nation was born in genocide. . . . We are perhaps the only nation which tried as a matter of national policy to wipe out its indigenous population. Moreover, we elevated that tragic experience into a noble crusade. Indeed, even

---

2. Part of the problem contributing to a limited view of salvation is Western Christianity's insistence on binary choices (i.e., divine/human, created/not created, Creator/Redeemer, Father/Son), which may be compounded in both the English language and Western logic. For example, in the Cherokee language we are able to use a phrase that points to Jesus as the *Creator-Son*. This linguistic construction references Jesus' sonship in relation to the Father, while at the same time referencing his role in creation. The word *son* in Cherokee is related to the word for egg. An egg is both chicken and egg at the same time. Respected Keetoowah Cherokee tradition keeper Thomas Belt and Margaret Bender write that "in Cherokee, one's child is *agwe:tsi*, 'my egg.' The child is inseparable from the speaker in two ways: first, a possessive pronoun is built into the word as a prefix (in this case in the form *agw-*, 'my') so that no child is an abstraction but is always the child of a specific person in a conversation; second, a child's biological origin as a part of the parent is reinforced throughout life since the word for child also means 'egg.'" Belt and Bender, "Speaking Difference to Power," 189.

When used with the word for Creator, the son becomes connected to the Creator through relationship and becomes indistinguishable from that relationship. In this simple linguistic formula Jesus is acknowledged as both divine Creator and divine Son. The implications of embracing broader understandings of Christ as the one who creates all things and as the one who restores all things has tremendous significance for the *missio Dei* as well as theological import. The God who creates all creation also sends, is sent to, and will restore all creation. Jesus, the Creator-Son, is one in indistinguishable relationship with God, sent by God.

today we have not permitted ourselves to reject
or to feel remorse for this shameful episode.[3]

When American theologians fail to understand and
acknowledge injustice concerning past, present, and continuous land thefts from America's host peoples, they do
not represent Christ well. When theologians fail to ask important theological questions of Indigenous peoples from
an open mind and heart, whole cultures and their values
can be and have been demeaned and destroyed in the name
of Christ's redeeming work. This theology or missiology
is actually based on a replacement model—replacing Indigenous theologies with Western theologies, which was
perhaps highlighted in the phrase "kill the Indian, save the
man." That was the popular thinking for almost a hundred
years of forced Indian assimilation into White culture
for tens of thousands of children in the US and Canada
through government/church-run residential Indian boarding schools. Indian children were beaten, brainwashed,
raped, and sodomized, and some even died in this grand
experiment, which was developed from a bad theology of
replacement and was eventually made into policy.

The failure of most Western theologians and missionaries to ask crucial questions demonstrates that they believed
the host peoples of this land had no stories worth hearing;
in other words, most Western theologies have shown they
believe that others, those who are different, have no viable
theology. In most cases theologians and missionaries too
often did not—and still do not—want to hear about Indigenous peoples' relationship with Creator. From the Western
perspective, if the indigenes had no stories of value, then the
only story worth telling was their own theologically biased,
Western story of Christ relating in their own Western culture.

3. King, "The Summer of Our Discontent," in *Why We Can't Wait*,
110.

They failed to realize that Indigenous peoples already possess a strong, creation-based theology.[4]

Bo: The boarding school era caused a lot of damage and disruption in the Native American community.

Randy: What I am proposing is that the Western, post-Enlightenment, modern, colonial worldview and theology has too often not brought people to a better understanding of Christ but has actually moved people further away from God's intended *shalom* reality made up of Christ's values. I am suggesting that the path of recovering a vital Christlike spirituality is to understand *shalom* through an alternative, postcolonial theological lens. People need to find Jesus in the deconstructive and reconstructive theological process and to live out Jesus' values through theologically demonstrated, shalom-based systems, not replacement theologies.

Real Land as Place, Not Space

Bo: Do you think most White Americans understand the damage that has been done by a replacement theology?

Randy: Actually, I do think they understand—they just don't want to talk about it. Colonialism is invariably associated with land theft. Land, and people's rightful place on the land, should mean something to those who understand its sacredness. In the Christian Scriptures and in most, if not all, Native American creation stories, the land is seen as sacred, usually as a gift from Creator. Good postcolonial theologies, then, should begin by first considering the sacredness of the earth and people's place on it. To do so

4. The prevalent, redemption-based emphasis of the Eurocentric missionaries might have diminished our own Native capacity to develop a contextual theology.

is to say to Creator that you appreciate the gift of life on earth and accept the fact that Indigenous peoples have a right to a particular land, and that land cannot simply be stolen through a show of power. It matters not your area of thought or expertise; it only matters that we begin at the ground level. I'm not suggesting that we begin with an abstract idea of earth but that we think about the actual ground under our feet. The ground under your feet, and the context of its bio-region, has a long history. The context of our own place on earth is both historic and social, as well as being religious/spiritual. The earth remembers all these aspects, as should we.

Bo: What do you think this kind of theological grounding can do differently for us?

Randy: Grounding ourselves helps to eliminate the horrid dualisms that are ever-present in Western society. Grounding ourselves makes life real. We are real persons, talking about and theologizing a real Jesus who lived, and lives, if you believe in spirit, on real earth. Keep your theology real. Keep your theology grounded. Keep your theology on earth. For Indigenous people, land has always been paramount in understanding Creator and how we are to live. Land not only gives us identity but it is often a part of the covenant story between the people and Creator. It is seen as both a gift and a responsibility for co-sustaining.

There is the strong community orientation among indigenes, reflecting a shalomlike worldview, which I refer to as the Harmony Way. Christians in the West who have propagated a theology that is antithetical to shalom, or harmonious coexistence, should begin to challenge their own individualistic worldview. Looking to the theologies of Indigenous peoples is one way to envision new postcolonial theologies. A cooperative culture, such as is found among most Indigenous peoples, as opposed to the more competitive culture found in the modern West, tends to share in activities and achievements with one another. Respect or tolerance and a deep understanding of diversity and consensus-making serve to make possible the uniqueness of the types of communities Jesus hoped we would make. These assumptions will even challenge our current views of democracy, our current government structures, and our philosophies built upon Western fallacies such as unbridled capitalism. When we understand life from an ethic of abundance and sharing, such as the one Jesus taught, there is no way one can be at ease with the current system of capitalism we now have in place.

Stolen Land

Bo: Interestingly, capital is gained through both labor and land. In the case of the United States, these were largely accrued by the unjust means of West African chattel slavery and the theft of Indigenous peoples' lands. How do we form any sort of righteous theology of the land with a history such as ours?

Randy: Granted, it's difficult for the West to form a righteous theology of place since the historical reality of America begins from a place of stolen land. Not that Christians haven't attempted to theologically justify their theft of the land and the massacres of Indian people from the very beginning. The fact that the West has a poorly developed (and in some cases entirely absent) theology of the land results in very abstract theologies that lack focus on particular lands or physical embodiment. That's where one of the most tragic dualisms comes in to play. Many Western theological constructs are, as a result, disembodied. A disembodied theology misses the point of incarnation and, while appearing to be ethical, lacks substance. As a result, those theologies must keep Jesus in his "rightful" place on the cross and avoid understanding him as Creator.

As Vine Deloria Jr. pointed out so very long ago in his book *God Is Red*, which really got this conversation started, the West puts an emphasis on time, which serves to replace actual place, location or land. *Place*, then, when thought of more in terms of time, takes on a more ethereal emphasis. Many traditional Native Americans understand the nature of Creator to be panentheistic. *Panentheism* is a constructed word from the Greek meaning "all-in-God," with the distinction made that while the world and universe are contained within God, God is greater than the whole of the universe and creation. From this position, there can be significant variation on how the relationship between God and creation plays out in a particular place. Bottom line, if you view the divine Spirit in everything, everything is sacred. Every place is sacred. The land itself is sacred. Given this worldview, one could not abuse the land or the people on the land without violating its sacredness. Time just does not have the same grounding. It's here and it's gone in a blink. Time gets to be "made-up," but place remains as a reminder regardless of how we choose to think of it.

Bo: So, in order to move Western theologies out of the abstract, how might settler-colonial Christianity begin with an honest theology of the land?

Randy: In his book about a similar situation in Australia, *Following Jesus in Invaded Space*, Christopher Budden posits the possibility that one's social location is the primary determinant of one's theology. Budden makes the point that unless Christians are willing to divest themselves of the wrong social location and its associated power, they cannot hope to create an honest theology of the land. As a result of having a postulated theology of the land, an alternative theological narrative must be constructed. Speaking of Australia Budden states,

> The church, the major holder of ultimate narrative, could find no place for the religious and social claims of Indigenous people. There was little sense that this was a people made in the image of God who could not then be made in the image of white people. There was no sense that this people may have been put on this land by God, or that this people already had some sense of God. There was none of the respect needed to treat Indigenous people as real neighbors, as the "other" whom the church needed to serve justly.[5]

The author draws his conclusions from the life of Jesus, expositing several New Testament texts that reinforce his ideas concerning social location, and then he delves into the way the European invasion has been fitted into a Western social construction of reality, resulting in a worldview that makes land theft seem normal. Budden defines racism theoretically and also in the particular context of Australia, which includes *White privilege* and *White normalcy*, two concepts well understood in critical race theory (CRT). He also suggests that the way forward is both structural and relational, requiring theological thought concerning the critical question, Where is God's presence and location found in a reconstructed theological narrative?

5. Budden, *Following Jesus in Invaded Space*, 33.

Land as Mythological Narrative

Like Australia, America has created a theological narrative based on ideas of freedom, equality, opportunity, and fairness. The imagined values even spin a narrative that props up the idea that America is the very place where the divine story uniquely comes together and unfolds as divine providence (à la Anglo-Saxon England, Dutch South Africa, etc., eh?). This mythical, divine grand narrative serves as the social location for the American Dream. The false narrative has become in a sense a real place, but the place is amorphous. Instead of *a particular land*, the Western mind tends to think in these terms: *the* land means *all* land. America, according to the American Dream sewn into the national myth, is the place of freedom, equality, opportunity, and fairness—not in any one place but "from sea to shining sea." The American Dream inherently contains an ethic of extreme competition, even to the point where Americans believe we must fight others (read: kill others) in order to be free and in order to retain our divinely bestowed values.

Bo: So, I'm guessing we might have grown up with differing ideas of what the American Dream means. Could you talk a bit more about how you see it and how it plays into our current theology?

Randy: Sure. We first have to ask, Who was it intended to energize and to what purpose? When I think of the phrase "the American Dream" I think of a time in the land before the invasion of Europeans. I think of a time before the largest demographic calamity in world history occurred on the North American continent, when more than one hundred million Indigenous North American people were wiped out by disease and planned genocide. I think of a time before the immoral, Christian Doctrine of Discovery justified the theft of whole continents, and before the Indian Removal Act, because of which thousands of Indians lost their lives while relocating so that Euro-Americans could steal Indian land. I think of mass movements in history such as Manifest Destiny that gave a nation justification, in the name of Jesus, to do whatever was necessary to Indigenous peoples in order to inhabit the land. I think of a time before Native American religions were outlawed and Native American culture was considered barbaric. When I think of the American Dream, I think of a time prior to the forced subjugation of tens of thousands of Native American children—more than five generations of children—who suffered inhumane treatment, torture, sexual abuse, cultural abuse, physical abuse, mental and spiritual abuse, and the general indignity of Native American boarding schools like Carlisle, Riverside, and Chemawa, the latter of which is located just down the highway from us in Salem, Oregon.

The epitome of what might be called the American Dream was no utopian vision but a lived, realized experience of striving toward harmony in this land. It was a time when what would become America was more culturally diverse, more religiously diverse, more ethnically diverse, more biologically diverse, healthier and more harmonious than any other time since. The American Dream I have read about, heard about from elders, and experienced just a portion of was not perfect. In fact, most of the inhabitants believed that striving for perfection was an offense to Creator. But there was likely never a war of religion fought here before 1492, nor one with the goal of colonizing or making one ethnic group in the cultural likeness of another. The time of which I speak was a time when diversity was seen as a strength and technological innovations were often shared freely. What I understand of my own personal Indigenous family story is germane to the concept of the American Dream.

Tocqua (near present-day Tellico, Tennessee) was the first village where I can trace my third great-grandfather living. He was Keetoowah—a Cherokee Indian. He was moved from there and, over the years, removed at least four more times, each time giving way to Euro-American land theft, justified by both the British and American governments. I know these places now. He knew them then: *Hickory Log*, near Canton, Georgia; *Squirrel Town*, near Trenton, Georgia; *Mill Creek*, in North Carolina; and eventually all the way to Indian Territory. *Gulequah* and his father, who, after becoming a prisoner, was killed by South Carolina militia during an escape attempt, were freedom fighters for the American Dream of which I speak. These are real places to me, not just history or time. The Chickamauga Cherokee fought for their people's freedom against the Americans in the longest war in American history, the Chickamauga War, which went from 1776 to 1795. My three times-great-grandfather was a signer of the first peace treaty between the US and Cherokee in 1791, and later he signed the Treaty of the Western Cherokee in 1817.

With each loss of a home, Gulequah's descendants grew in their imposed poverty, and in my grandmother's words, who married one of those descendants, "they never had time for grass to grow under their feet." Those descendants became several generations of coal miners in northern Alabama, where, for most of their lives, they hardly saw the sunlight. Unfortunately, as is often the case, those who are most exploited end up exploiting others. My mother's ancestors could only find work in the most extremely harsh and menial jobs where they had to exploit the earth for her coal. Later, Edward Broadhead, my mother's father, fought the corporate giants at Lehigh Coal in order to establish the

United Mine Workers in central Alabama. As a result, they eventually moved from being considered a tool, little better than a pick or a shovel in the eyes of the company, to becoming more like human beings again. Even with those strides, theirs was no American Dream.

Bo: That's a pretty sad and thought-provoking story.

Randy: I suppose, since I have the privilege of being a first-generation college student and holding a PhD, someone could say, "See, they worked hard, and you have attained the American Dream as a result!" And there was a time I might have acquiesced to such a notion. In 2004 my wife, Edith, and our family started a Native American ministry and cultural renewal center in old Cherokee territory near Lexington, Kentucky. On those fifty acres we had a farm; we invested our life's savings to build roads and buildings and barns; there were pastures and orchards, and we developed springs. We were conducting incredible schools with around forty people. But at the height of our success, the county denied our legal permit to build sleeping cabins for our students. In fact, about thirty of our neighbors showed up to protest our presence and intentions. This was followed by a White supremacist paramilitary group firing daily a 50-caliber machine gun on our property line, to kill us or to threaten us—we at first did not know which. In our plight, we could get no help from the Department of Justice, nor from the Fair Housing Council, nor from the state's attorney general, nor from the county sheriff's department. We had to refinance our home twice to stay afloat and finally were forced to sell it at half its appraised value during the economic downturn, just to keep our family safe. This high-stress situation took a toll not only on our financial stability, wiping out in one fell swoop our life's savings and earned equity, but it also took a serious toll on our family. And this is just one experience of one Native American family who tried to "make it" in America's dreamland. Now, is that what you think of when you hear the words "American Dream"?

I want to pull a quote from one of my former professor's books. Howard Snyder, in *Jesus and Pocahontas: Gospel, Mission and National Myth*, writes,

> Pocahontas portrayals . . . tell the saga of Indian-white relations. At first the Indians are hostile and dangerous. But key figures like Pocahontas bring reconciliation. Eventually the Indians are subdued and (according to the myth) integrated into the new nation. From the first, two options loomed for the Indians: peaceful integration on the white man's terms (symbolized by Pocahontas's marriage and baptism), or forced submission, marginalization, or annihilation. . . . Pocahontas speaks . . . of the stealing of native lands and the genocide of native peoples—America's original sin. Though well known and fully documented, this sin's moral meaning *has never been faced.* The scattered impoverished Indian reservations sprinkled helter-skelter across the landscape, plus the underclass of Native Americans in many large US cities, bear contemporary witness.[6]

The American Dream, which I believe may be the deepest-held religion in America, promises the future hope of security, salvation, development, civilization, equality, freedom, and prosperity. But what is actually delivered to those who cannot assimilate into the unstated, darker values of American society is imbalance, oppression, violence, and destruction.

6. Snyder, *Jesus and Pocahontas*, 153–54, 213.

As long as the American Dream continues to be built upon the foundation of threat, fear, violence, theft, murder, rape, torture, and selfish greed, all absorbed into a mythological denial of fact and truth, it cannot by any means be called a dream (especially by those who claim to follow Jesus); rather, it is an American Horror Story—a nightmare! The American Dream attempts to justify itself by its outlier success stories, much like lottery winners, but if you are not White, and you cannot assimilate into the patterns, values, and goals of White normalcy, you will most often fail to achieve the American Dream. Such a utopian vision ultimately justifies its means by its end, but that is not the way of Christ, right? Jesus said, let your yes be yes, and your no be no. The dualism and utopianism so pervasive in American Christianity aids the ungodly means of White supremacy by elevating the spiritual over the physical, becoming like the Greeks, the Romans, the British, the South Africans, and so many other nations who have also justified their despotic means by the end goal.

As we can see, this false narrative of the American Dream has not brought most Americans the promises of God as found in Jesus' shalom government. Instead, the American Dream has supported genocide, slavery, classism, racism, genderism, sexism, ableism, and the exploitation of the poor and marginalized, in this country and in others. Perhaps above all else, in order to maintain our "American Dream," the United States has incorporated an ethic of continuous war. Racism, sexism, ableism, etc., work against the shalom values found in diversity. The exploitation of the poor and the marginalized is the very opposite of the shalom empire of love. War and the illegitimate use of power target, exploit, and destroy one's enemy as opposed to loving one's enemy. The task of scholars touting this theologized American Myth is to find historical, theological, or philosophical loopholes or rationalizations for war and other such anti-Christ actions, but the task of true Jesus followers is to confront and condemn such actions with a grounded understanding of what love means.

Concluding Remarks

Bo: Okay, maybe we should try to recap?

Randy: The conquest of land and the resources that amount to capital—and ultimately power—which are contained on, in, and through the land, are the initial goals of colonization and what has been called the American Dream. This dream substitutes for an American theology of the land. And let us not forget that cruel force was used to obtain these goals. The militarization of the Western mind has become part and parcel of the national mythos—and, unfortunately, the envy and "dream" of many other nations. Justice, when it comes to imperial military logic, has very little bearing, and thus it means little in American theology. The occupying military force in the land that eventually became the United States of America has barely seen a handful of years without military conflict. This in turn has created a culture of violence and has had a tremendous effect on the American psyche and America's policies at home and abroad. Competition, the misuse of power, violence, and division have become the new normal, and Evangelical

Christians all over America have now apparently bought into it. Part of the reason Americans are always in conflict is that Americans are satisfied with a myth that has created a false sense of shalom.

Americans—and Evangelicals in particular, I should add—feel as if they already have a divine sense of purpose and the divine destiny God promises, so instead of looking to God for a true model of harmony, Americans feed their own sense of false harmony by robbing the poor and marginalized in order to maintain the present military model that supports their American Dream. The model served by American nationalism is built on conflict, militarism, and most often greed—not shalom—and this model, by any standard of fairness, has not served Jesus' shalom kingdom well.

The mechanisms of war, trade, and diplomacy that continue to drain Indigenous and other people of the world of their natural and other resources are not maintained solely through military conquest. Global trade agreements, trade embargoes, and "diplomatic" political pressure maintain the economic and political neocolonial strongholds of military and economic colonial nations over less empowered nations. In many ways, the pressure and dependency that other nations feel, including our Indigenous nations in America, is just as dehumanizing as military defeat. Unhealthy dependencies upon the super-powerful develop to the point where seemingly weaker nations are forced to take unjust loans (through institutions such as the World Bank and International Monetary Fund), block grants, and food, health and housing assistance. What Western nations call democratic capitalism is perhaps now one of the most oppressive forces in history, and it has been assembled through neocolonialism.

Bo: Can you talk about what you think of theologically when you refer to neocolonialism?

Randy: World powers demand stable global economies in order to make a profit and therefore must pressure other nations, through neocolonialism's many tentacles, to give in to imbalanced trade deals, unjust loans, immoral political alliances and dependencies that are often not in their own best interest. When those with less economic and political power do not cooperate, they must choose to suffer illegitimate power plays, sanctions, or even coups to bring them in line. Ultimately, these nations, which are already poor and under-resourced, having likely had most of their resources stolen by the more "powerful" nations, are forced to suffer the dehumanization of poor health, lack of economic opportunities, and the disintegration of their communities. The stories of those whose lives are affected by neocolonialism—children in Indonesia chained to trees while slaving in the palm oil industry, for example, or women in Central America working for a dollar a day to produce roses for Valentine's Day—only rarely make it into newspapers in the West.

I want to play a song for you, if you are not familiar with it. Perhaps the poet/songwriter Bruce Cockburn is better at describing the reality of democratic capitalism's neocolonial impact in his song "Call It Democracy." Here are a few lines:

> Padded with power here they come
> International loan sharks backed by the guns
> Of market-hungry military profiteers
> Whose word is a swamp and whose brow is smeared
> With the blood of the poor
>
> Sinister cynical instrument
> Who makes the gun into a sacrament

The only response to the deification
Of tyranny by so-called "developed" nations'
Idolatry of ideology

See the paid-off local bottom feeders
Passing themselves off as leaders
Kiss the ladies shake hands with the fellows
Open for business like a cheap bordello

And they call it Democracy[1]

Bo: Powerful words!

Randy: With such a historical record of the illegitimate use of military and neocolonial power deeply woven into modern Western theology, Americans cannot make any honest claim concerning justice or freedom or an American Dream that rests on equality. We do not have shalom! Instead, the words of the ancient Hebrew prophets come to mind: "They offer superficial treatments for my people's mortal wound. They give assurances of peace when there is no peace" (Jer 6:14 NLT). On the other hand, before the arrival of the Europeans, hundreds of North American Native nations were able to live near one another and trade with each other with much less conflict than we have seen since the invasion of America. This was due to the Harmony Way values, including the many peacemaking strategies employed by America's Indigenous peoples.

Theologians of empire have explicitly and implicitly condoned a colonial theology of conquest by justifying war and military might or by simply not confronting it with a postcolonial theology that reflects the words and teachings

1. Bruce Cockburn, "Call It Democracy," from *World of Wonders* (1986). Reprinted by permission.

of Jesus Christ. The illegitimate use of power dehumanizes and demeans both the oppressed and the oppressor. In the end, both sides suffer from inhumane treatment by understanding themselves as less human than they were created to be. In both the oppressed and the oppressor, the inhumanity they feel, whether acknowledged or not, leads to a series of maladies that beset them throughout their lives and linger for generations to come. After generations of these twisted acts, and in the face of the rippling repercussions, the need for postcolonial theologians becomes more crucial than ever. But speaking truth to power is never easy.

Postcolonial theologies must touch the deepest places in individual hearts and the most complex systems of societal structure. A postcolonial theologian must spend time not only deconstructing the colonizing lies of others but also engaging in personal examination, asking how she herself has bought into the lies and how she cooperates with those existing systemic structures. She must delve deep in her research and study especially the many historical narratives available from people on all sides of an event or issue so that she can understand better where Jesus stands and make her stand with Christ.

Every area of society is up for critique, deconstruction and reconstruction, including wealth and poverty, military actions and budgets, immigration, trade policies, safety nets for the poor, tax structures, the rights of disenfranchised peoples—women, people of color, the LGBTQ community, immigrants, Indigenous peoples—and the ecological crisis. In a society such as ours, and in a modern world founded on and immersed in colonial practices of injustice and the use of illegitimate power, the postcolonial theologian must sacrifice much in order to serve Christ effectively.

It is in real-life struggles and in listening to the voices of the people who are themselves struggling against the illegitimate use of power that the answers to our theological questions are most often found. Ultimately, the postcolonial theologian will find that she too is concerned with justifying the use of power—but her theological rationale is primarily concerned with how to *empower* others by ensuring that those who have not been heard gain the dignity of voice.

Bibliography

Anderson, Benedict R. O'G. *Imagined Communities: Reflections on the Origin and Spread of Nationalism.* London: Verso, 1983.

Belt, Thomas, and Margaret Bender. "Speaking Difference to Power: The Importance of Linguistic Sovereignty." In *Foundations of First Peoples' Sovereignty: History, Education & Culture*, edited by Ulrike Wiethaus, 187–96. New York: P. Lang, 2008.

Bevans, Stephen B. *Models of Contextual Theology.* Rev. ed. Maryknoll, NY: Orbis, 2002.

Budden, Christopher. *Following Jesus in Invaded Space: Doing Theology on Aboriginal Land.* Eugene, OR: Pickwick, 2009.

Césaire, Aimé. *Discourse on Colonialism.* Translated by Joan Pinkham. New York: Monthly Review, 2000.

Deloria, Vine, Jr. *God Is Red.* New York: Grosset & Dunlap, 1973.

Dube, Musa W. *Postcolonial Feminist Interpretation of the Bible.* St. Louis: Chalice, 2000.

Eagleton, Terry. *After Theory.* New York: Basic Books, 2004. Kindle.

Eastman, Charles A. Ohiyesa. *The Soul of the Indian.* 1911. Reprint, New York: Dover, 2003.

Fanon, Frantz. *Black Skin, White Masks.* Translated by Charles Lam Markmann. New York: Grove, 1967.

———. *The Wretched of the Earth.* Translated by Constance Farrington. New York: Grove Weidenfeld, 1963.

King, Martin Luther, Jr. *Why We Can't Wait.* New York: Signet Classic, 2000.

McClaren, Brian. "Post-Colonial Theology." January 31, 2011. http://www.redletterchristians.org/post-colonial-theology/.

McDonough, Sean M. *Christ as Creator: Origins of a New Testament Doctrine.* Oxford: Oxford University Press, 2009.

Nelson, Cary, and Lawrence Grossberg. *Marxism and the Interpretation of Culture.* Urbana: University of Illinois Press, 1988.

Quijano, Aníbal, and Immanuel Wallerstein. "Americanity as a Concept; or, the Americas in the Modern World-System." *International Social Science Journal* 44 (1992) 549–57.

Saldívar, José David, ed. *Trans-Americanity: Subaltern Modernities, Global Coloniality, and the Cultures of Greater Mexico.* Durham: Duke University Press, 2012.

Schillebeeckx, Edward. *The Church with a Human Face: A New and Expanded Theology of Ministry.* Translated by John Bowden. New York: Crossroad, 1985.

Smith, Andrea. "Indigeneity, Settler Colonialism, White Supremacy." 2011. https://www.calfac.org/sites/main/files/file-attachments/andy_smith_indigeneity_settler_colonialism_white_supremacy.pdf.

Snyder, Howard. *Jesus and Pocahontas: Gospel, Mission, and National Myth.* Eugene, OR: Cascade, 2015.

Sugirtharajah, R. S., ed. *Asian Faces of Jesus.* Maryknoll, NY: Orbis, 1993.

———. *Exploring Postcolonial Biblical Criticism: History, Method, Practice.* Malden, MA: Wiley-Blackwell, 2012.

———. *Postcolonial Criticism and Biblical Interpretation.* Oxford: Oxford University Press, 2002.

———, ed. *Voices from the Margin: Interpreting the Bible in the Third World.* London: SPCK, 1991.

Taylor, Charles. *Modern Social Imaginaries.* Durham: Duke University Press, 2004.

West, Cornel, with David Ritz. *Brother West: Living and Loving Out Loud; a Memoir.* New York: SmileyBooks, 2009.

Whitehead, Alfred North. *Process and Reality: An Essay in Cosmology.* Edited by David Ray Griffin and Donald W. Sherburne. Corrected ed. New York: Free Press, 1978.

Woodley, Randy. *Shalom and the Community of Creation: An Indigenous Vision.* Grand Rapids: Eerdmans, 2012.

———. *When Going to Church Is Sin and Other Essays on Native American Christian Missions.* Scotland, PA: Healing the Land, 2007.

Young, Robert J. C. *Postcolonialism: A Very Short Introduction.* Oxford: Oxford University Press, 2003.

Made in the USA
Monee, IL
09 August 2020